FOOD:
AN APPETITE
FOR LIFE

Adria L. Libolt

Food: An Appetite for Life Copyright © 2018 by Adria Libolt. All rights reserved. Printed in the United States of America. No part of this book may be reproduced or transmitted in any form or by any means, electronic or mechanical, including photocopying, recording or by any information storage, and retrieval system without written permission from the author or publisher. For information, contact White Bird Publications, LLC.

Visit our website at www.whitebirdpublications.com

ISBN: 978-1-63363-329-2
LCCN: 2018964812

To Clay

who has an appetite for good food and shares my hunger for life

Acknowledgments

I am thankful to all those who fed me through the years: for the times spent in the kitchen with Mom, where I received advice (often unsolicited) about cooking and other matters; for fresh trout for breakfast from Dad; for my parents' prayers and blessings. I'm thankful for meals as a guest at the tables of brothers and sisters, and for all the family and friends who made meals for me and spoke the language of food.

Thanks also go to the friends and family who were guests at my table when I experimented, when a meal didn't turn out the way I planned, when I burned the potatoes, underdid the meat, or forgot to serve the dishes I left in the back of the refrigerator—in other words, when the porridge was too hot or too cold.

I'm especially grateful to my editor Ulrike Guthrie for her encouraging words and comments about food, a few times urging me to take uncompromising stands and insist on wholesome, unadulterated food, and for her exceptional and skillful editing that brought this book to this point. I am most fortunate to know her. The infelicities and misstatements that remain are, of course, my own, as is the poetry and all recipes (unless noted).

Evelyn Byrne-Kusch at White Bird, writer and publisher, has been insightful, encouraging, and kind. With her suggestions and ideas, she has made this book a reality and in doing so made it much more satisfying and delectable for hungry readers.

I owe much to my creative, loving husband, a writer, and pastor who encourages me, and who is hungry for food and life, likes and loves what I cook, sometimes for the sheer love of me, eats leftovers, tolerates the cooking experiments, and God be praised, is still healthy.

CONTENTS

HUNGRY FOR EVERYTHING: THE PATOIS OF FOOD

Our plates are piled high with a culture of food: food fashion in the media, losing and gaining weight, choices, changes, and the contradictions and discrepancies between rich and poor. Do we choose wisely?

The Bible uses the language of food to describe the fullness of life. Sometimes we define abundance narrowly as possessions. Our limitations keep us from seeking and experiencing hunger that enriches our lives. Memories at a table whet an appetite for life beyond the good food.

Chapter 1 Hungry for Everything and a Taste of Fullness

THE LANGUAGE OF PROMISING EATING TRENDS: CREATIVITY, FORAGING, AND SMALL PLATES: Chapters 2-5

Creativity with food can be extreme, artistic, and lead to new ways with food. Foraging and living with what our earth produces and what foods grow around us in the wild may give us what's fresh and simple without transportation and processing. Small plates provide a variety of tastes and satisfy smaller appetites for sedentary lifestyles. Chapters 2-4 discuss these trends.

Chapter 2 Playing with Food: Smearing, Foaming, Loafing and Lab-Grown
Experimenting and creating foods in the lab can produce food in new ways—faux foods which may be substituted for meat or chemical food. Creative and stylish food captivates but may become a means to an end—beautiful, dramatic, yet impractical food that doesn't have much taste or nutritional value.

Chapter 3 Foragers
Foraging is an attractive idea for finding what's growing locally and seasonally. It harkens back to an innocence that is refreshing though not always practical.

Chapter 4 Nibble without a Quibble
Small portions, appetizers or tapas, eaten slowly over time are satisfying. When we don't want to take the time or can't wait, we indulge in big bites.

Chapter 5 Finger Foods—The Right Touch
Though we often eat food with our fingers/finger foods, we have lost touch with where and how and by whom food is grown. The Lord's Supper is a sacrament of remembering and has the potential to remind us of our dependence on the land and each other.

WORDS OF FOOD ADVICE: Chapters 6-11

Chapter 6   Sgt. Peppers
Some of the best advice about food comes from neighbors and friends, and sometimes we can get too much of both good food and advice.

Chapter 7   A Middle Eastern Lunch: An Opinion Comes with That
Sometimes food seems to come with well-intended advice, and we're faced with accepting the food even if we can't accept the advice. Some cultures assume we share their values as we often assume when visiting other countries.

Chapter 8   Beef for Real and Sausage
When asked, a butcher offers simple advice, from baking meat slowly in three ingredients to grilling a peanut butter sandwich. His homemade andouille sausage was a delicious complex mixture, in contrast to his plain philosophy that claims fat is satisfying.

Chapter 9   Turkeys—Cheep and Cheaper
Poultry is made available cheaply at holidays, but we cannot ignore the costs some poultry workers pay for processing and getting poultry to our tables cheaply.

Chapter 10   Bûche de Noël
On holidays we cook different dishes and concoctions and bake differently, adding to the anxiety of the season. Baked cakes, cookies, and other desserts can be challenging, but can look like works of art, becoming Christmas presents to each other and ourselves.

Chapter 11   Ollie Bollen on New Year's Day
A New Year's tradition brings sweet memories of traditional Ollie Bollen, a parent's advice, and advice in old recipe books.

FOOD ACCIDENTS—THE GOOD, BAD, AND EDIBLE: Chapters 12-15

Chapter 12   Mixing, Matching, and Accidents: The Grammar of What Works
Some foods are mixed together accidentally and make good combinations, while others seem to be thrown together and have less harmony with each other. But then, should food be feng shui?

Chapter 13   A Near Ruin by Ruam: Smoke and the Dark Side of Food
Too much of a good thing—like food coloring, garlic, smoke, or fire—can ruin a good meal. Fired and smoked food are best barbequed outside in the open air.

Chapter 14   Shaping A Signature Dish: More on Hamburger

We shape and mold food and experiment. We may not think about how we are shaped by what we eat, or how we shape our world by what we eat.

Chapter 15   The Luck of the Pot—Can We Trust our Food?

We depend on our food industry to feed large numbers of people, but poisons, chemicals, processing, and transportation compromise our land and food. Access and distribution may prevent healthy food from reaching those who need it. Some are hungry and malnourished. We eat potluck from our food industry. Can we trust it to feed everyone? What are our choices?

WAITING, RECEIVING, and SERVING: Food's Language: Chapters 16-21

Chapter 16   Martha and Mary

Hospitality is a relationship of serving and being served. We are both guests and those who wait on others. Food is a gift received and can bring us together over tables where we speak love to the loneliness and violence in our world.

Chapter 17   Serving Food

Family style evening meals at college brought students together weeknights in a coerced arrangement, seated next to each other, boy-girl. Serving strange students meals in that setting was uncomfortable but preferable to eating family style. It was a time of hunger for food and life.

Chapter 18   The Table

Tables are important. Life can be intense at tables where hunger exposes emotions. We grow when facing others for meals. Reconciliation can happen around tables.

Chapter 19   Waiting on Diners

Good wait staff are formal, informal, and knowledgeable about the food they serve. They can make one feel as though one is eating in luxury.

Chapter 20   Food: A Language Insisting on Freedom

Having someone prepare a meal is a gift that can make us feel blessed. We remember the people who are forced to make meals in depressing circumstances or dangerous places, and who still affirm life by serving others in hope.

Chapter 21   Wildly Eating Each Other

What is raised and killed to eat is often a matter of taste and culture. Eating may not be appealing if we become too familiar with the word-less wild or non-human animal. Wild or raised, humans are gobbling up a variety of animals and, in some countries, more than enough protein.

MEMORIES AND ASSOCIATIONS—Coming of Age and Food Fighting: Chapters 22-29

Chapter 22 The Palate of Place
Foods come with memories and are associated with places, events, and family. Children have food fights but passion about foods today results in more grown-up controversies. Food can be the site of both personal denial and indulgence.

Chapter 23 Food from Heaven—the Potato
Some staples like potatoes are favorites in many cultures. Nigerians raise and prepare a delicious yam in the country that is the yam capital of the world.

Chapter 24 One Potato, Two Potato: More on Potatoes

Potatoes prepared in different ways are a rich tradition linked to a heritage. Potatoes were usually part of the meal. Only the meat changed.

Chapter 25 Cracking Open Eggs
Eggs are the food language of fragility, easy to break, impossible to mend. Growing up or beginning anew entails necessary changes, brokenness, and messiness in life. Cleaning eggs led to negative associations and a child's aversion to them.

Chapter 26 Strawberries
Picking strawberries stained our hands and clothes and left indelible memories of delicious berries, hard work, and berry fights. Earning money was part of picking too.

Chapter 27 The Milky Way—Cream of the Crop
Assumptions we made in the past about some foods, like milk and dairy, have changed because of new findings, additives to food, and allergies. Controversies lead to food "fights" as adults.

Chapter 28 Eating and Food Disorders
Food nourishes, but some people eat or don't eat to satisfy psychological needs.

Chapter 29 Eating: Public and Private, Hide and Seek Food
Foods are both denied and used in excess. Today many meals are consumed alone. Does eating together prevent or cure some disorders that have occurred in private?

EATING ABROAD—GUESTS IN POOR COUNTRIES: Chapters 30-32

Chapter 30 Hospitality in Haiti and Abundance in Nigeria
Jesus didn't talk about scarcity, but feasting, celebrating, and abundance. Abundance is what is plentiful, but not necessarily in the possessions we accumulate or the things we purchase.

Chapter 31 Haiti—Light and Hospitality
Haiti has experienced many hardships. People work hard on projects to sustain themselves. Evidence of people's faith is everywhere and attracts visitors and people in development who work with the Haitians.

Chapter 32 Snap Judgments in Nigeria
In poor countries, we can be overwhelmed if our vision is too small when looking at the large pictures of needs. Focusing on what is in front of us and being a guest and learning from Nigerians made it possible to form friendships and partnerships.

FOOD FOR THE SOUL: THE LANGUAGE OF REST: Chapters 33-37

Chapter 33 Sabbatical in Iona and France
A retreat or rest is important for the soul and getting away from work and home makes it possible to gain new perspectives while enjoying foods in different settings.

Chapter 34 Soul Food—the Isle of Iona
Going to Iona was a pilgrimage. Some places seem more sacred than others and fill us with awe. Services at the abbey and the food were heavenly. But the life of monks is hard and feeling spiritual is not the same as being spiritual. Christ is not confined to places we find sacred but, on the move, and in wretched places, too. We are the salt of the earth, even in ordinary places.

Chapter 35 Looking for Lou Pistou
A small French restaurant with fresh, delicious food filled our evening, and the customers and wait staff were gracious. It was not a place to eat and run.

Chapter 36 Lunch at Versailles: Let us Eat Cake
Physical needs at a luxurious historical site brought us from the glitter of gold back to a common city street and rustic hospitality of the French—true luxury.

Chapter 37 The Last French Bite: The Skinny on Eating
The way we eat, what we eat, and the width of our streets may all have an impact on our weight.

Preface

This Is Just to Say

I have eaten the plums that were in the icebox
—William Carlos Williams

I wrote this book about food and eating because, like MFK Fisher, I am hungry for life. I learned early that food is best when served up in the company of others along with stories, conversations, and laughter. I grew up at tables like that. I learned at these tables a longing for the abundant life, an on-going hunger. In this book, I tell stories about meals I've served and meals that have been served to me at tables near and far. Food is the language of longing, shared together.

This is a book of reflective, sometimes passionate essays about food—the food itself, cooking it, and eating it. However, our hunger is for more than food: it is for the goodness of life and friendship itself. Turn the pages, and you are in a kitchen with family or friends preparing Chicken Marsala or cooking a meal when suddenly the kitchen fills with smoke. A stir-fry recipe best cooked outdoors follows the story. You will discover along with me experiments that flop, and how the flops sometime lead to just the sort of fun that is the essence of community—stories and food coming together like bread and butter.

You will stand in a field watching a juicy strawberry fight, followed by a recipe that uses the same berries in a better way. You will be led to reflect on how memory—the vivid memories of simple foods like eggs, milk, and potatoes—and how culture and style all have an impact on what we eat.

You will be led to ponder the significance of tables, happiness as well as sadness at the table, and how eating can become as complicated as a well-made soufflé and as varied as vegetables in a stew.

In the book, finger foods, as well as large and meaty dishes, come with a serving of advice on the plate. I reflect on the way one lingers on food in France, on eating small plates, and on eating quickly and alone in our own culture. Elsewhere I dine with others, eating pounded yam or coleslaw with catsup on top, and wonder about the irony of abundance, and how and why we eat the way we do.

This book began with little pieces meant to be as light as a soufflé and as easygoing as plucking a plum from a tree or, even easier, from a bowl in the refrigerator. I began writing these essays to entertain my writing group. But food (and the way we eat) like life itself is often complicated, messy, half-baked, sour, and bitter. Life is spinach caught in the teeth while interviewing for a job. Nevertheless, flops in the kitchen are humorous and harmless compared to the ways that we now alter food with grim consequences for our health. Worse, food can become hard to get, to grow, or to harvest, and when we get it, comes laden with pesticides, other poisons, useless calories, and unnecessary additives. It is not as easy as baking an airy soufflé first appears. Hunger and eating are complicated topics.

Soufflés are only light if they rise properly. I know a man who blamed his oven when his soufflés weren't coming out right and replaced it for one with a more reliable temperature control. To be right, a soufflé must expand and stay puffed up before it's eaten, or it's not a soufflé but its common third cousin, scrambled eggs.

When I was younger, I assumed everyone ate the way I did: around a table, after a prayer, food home grown, fish locally caught—all of it rich and abundant. I had a child's limited view in a more innocent time about food and eating. In this book, my joys and my foibles related to food mix with an expanded awareness that what comes on our plates can no longer be eaten innocently like children but requires us to make choices that have consequences for justice, health, our culture, and our communities.

In these small essays, I also reflect on how food is portrayed in the media, on food as fashion, on how writing and talking about food ripen into unwanted advice and unsolicited judgment as many of us claim expertise in food and diets. I raise on-going concerns about the industrialization of food while, at the same time, inquiring about ways to feed our populated earth. I ask how some can have at their disposal such a variety and abundance of food while others do not have enough. Even slight exposure to what goes on in the food world and a bit of knowledge forces on us an awareness of others' hunger. Is talk of austerity a response to waste? Greed? A fear of scarcity? What are the consequences of how we eat?

There are other questions on my table too. The book explores some of the craziness, extremes, and disorders of our food culture. The first chapter covers some of the language, conflicting messages and controversies, and my deliberations and hesitations as I consider what to cook and eat for one meal. I realize how easy it is to become obsessive about food rather than appreciating what we have and hungering for the fullness and goodness of life.

Daily experiences of food and eating and of taking time to pause or pray became for me moments to think about our condition and that of our land, water, and air, and what it means to sit at tables, waiting on others and being served. I explore how the hunger of the body reminds us of the common ground of our souls, about tasting milk and honey, including the milk and honey that are the desires and promise of the sweetness of the best of life. I describe how food traditions connect us to our families and our pasts, and how the memories of certain foods continue to have an impact on our lives. The book talks about how we depend on each other when traveling in other countries, and how the language of hunger encourages us to be patient visitors and courteous guests.

Above all, I hope to convey the wonder of food. Good food is always a substantial gift and a cause for celebration and joy. I hope you are hungry for more and will join me here to see what it is like at my table.

Oh, and this book includes a few short prayers and poems and recipes, including this simple soufflé.

Simple Soufflé
4 servings

3 tablespoons milk
½ teaspoon salt
Ground fresh pepper
4 egg yolks at room temperature
4 egg whites at room temperature
½ cup grated Gruyere, optional
3 tablespoons butter

Preheat oven to 375 degrees.
1. Separate yolks and beat them until thick and lemon colored, and add the milk, salt, and pepper.
2. In a separate bowl, beat egg whites until stiff but not dry.
3. Pour egg yolk mixture into egg whites, folding very gently until blended.
4. Butter an eight-inch cast iron pan.
5. Turn the egg mixture into the pan spreading evenly.
6. Cook slowly about 5 minutes on low-medium.
7. When puffed and slightly browned, place in oven at 375 degrees for about 8 minutes or until top is browned.
8. Serve with cheese or fruit.

1

Hungry for Everything and a Taste of Fullness

God grant me the serenity to accept the things I ought to eat,
The courage to avoid the things I shouldn't eat…
And the wisdom to know
that a little chocolate never hurt anyone.

We are both free diners and prisoners of the table of our time.[1]

While driving I am listening to Lynn Rosetta Caspar on National Public Radio tell us that her show is for people who like to eat. She is talking to me. She describes the pasta alfredo and crème brûlée with never a mention of the calories.

---
[1] (Gopnik 2011, 107)

I wait in line at the grocery store. Skimming the magazines, I see a picture of the late James Beard with his ruddy cheeks and smile. In other magazines, movie stars provide their recipes for how they slimmed down, losing and keeping off fifty pounds of fat, their stories complete with before and after pictures. I see articles on the best ice cream sundae and brownies. I read about Maria who got into her swimsuit after trying to medicate her postpartum blues with chocolate cookies. All while standing at the checkout, I read about the foods that are good for us, the foods that help us lose weight and gain weight, and what foods are popular.

Then there are the foods that go in and out of fashion. Is steak in or out? If it's grass-fed and has more of the omega fats we need, is it better? Didn't we have margarine, so we wouldn't eat butter, and now we are cautious about what type of margarine we eat and read that butter is in? I like the "but only" advice: that carbohydrates are in again *but only* if they are the right kinds like brown rice and whole grains. Some fats, like those found in nuts, are healthy *but only* if they are indulged in sparingly. A little sweetness is all right, *but only* if we don't eat too much refined sugar. Recent news says sugar is dangerous and responsible for obesity (Engber 2017). Fashion suggests foods that are cool—or hot—depending on what's in style today.

Spices, herbs, and sauces take a back seat to other "hot" products that come on the market. Once there was Tabasco. Now there is also Garam Masala, Chipotle, Smoked Paprika, Sriracha, Aleppo Pepper, and Sambal Oelek.

Can anyone keep up with the latest fat-burners and fountains of youth? Move over green tea. Dr. Oz is recommending green coffee beans. But don't buy too large a quantity: something will replace them tomorrow.

And that food pyramid. What's on top of it now? Is meat shrinking? Vegetables expanding?

What's a woman or man to do?

Grocery stores have changed in the last few years. Many stores have sections of gluten-free foods and some whole aisles. Many packages of food now carry labels of "gluten-free." I know some people are seriously allergic to gluten, but I wonder whether others may have confused gluten with glutton. I grew up hearing that Jesus is the Bread of Life. What would Jesus eat today?

Gluten may sound akin to gut and gluttony, but according to Dr. Amy Myers (Myers 2013) and others, celiac disease and gluten intolerance have increased over the last fifty years from one in 650 to one in 120 people. The disease is associated with wheat proteins, some of which have been added to the wheat to make our wheat grow faster and be drought and pest-resistant. These proteins can lead to inflammation, gluten intolerance, and celiac disease. Some people have developed an immune response to the wheat. Exacerbating this is that more and more foods and other products now unnecessarily contain gluten—think some French Fries and Tater Tots, cheeses, toothpastes, and potato chips, as well as countless sauces and condiments. So, in answer to my question: What *would* Jesus eat? After all, in the past, Jesus, the Bread of Life ate the natural wheat growing in the area and other unprocessed foods, and bread referred to the needs and hunger of the soul just as often as it did actual food.

In our stores, not only do we have choices of wheat and gluten-free breads, but many choices of produce and dairy foods too. The food carts waiting in checkout lanes show our choices, and that what we eat is related to fashion. Think about the foods your parents or grandparents ate and what you eat. I remember a time when ham slices on white buns or Wonder bread ("building bodies twelve ways") and green Jell-O were served in the churches I attended, but then other foods replaced them. Adam Gopnik, in *The Table Comes First*, claims that taste is tied to social change and asks who is likely to eat brown bread, local vegetables, free-range chicken, and raw milk cheese: farmers' great-grandchildren or professors of comparative literature? (Gopnik 2011, 91-93) The penny casserole I made in college, like a war-time spam dish, with slices of wieners swimming in a stew of potatoes and canned soup would not win any prizes for being fashionable or nutritious. The food police would come for me. There are worse offenses. I hope that those eating shark fin soup will find their taste for it unfashionable before sharks disappear. Certainly, snobbishness supplements food talk about what's stylish, so some look askance at using cake mixes or cream of mushroom soup as unhealthy or so yesterday. We are eager to be food trendy with fresh food and quick to judge others whose food choices seem passé. Processed, imperishable, and canned and preserved foods are often shunned and donated to food banks for those who can't afford the better stuff.

I volunteered at a local community assistance program. One of the volunteers reported that a woman who had been offered food from the food bank requested grocery money instead for steaks. She did not fancy the bags of rice and dried beans and canned food offered at the food bank. When I heard this, several judgmental thoughts ran through my mind: Beans and rice are *better* for you. Don't you *know* how to cook beans and rice? Oh, perhaps you don't have a stove (not everyone does.) *You* are ungrateful. Beggars can't be choosers.

But why would we judge people in need of food in a worse light than we'd judge people who consume unsustainable rare foods like shark fins or those who overindulge in expensive foods (steaks), and who could eat the more simple rice and beans? Those in need of food know our culture too. They know about trendy eating and styles. Many know to ask for gluten-free foods and ask why they should be satisfied with bags of beans when they know the people who donate them may be having steak instead.

What we write about food may also go out of style. Daily articles and studies report conflicting advice about what and how we should eat to stay healthy. I know that what I'm writing now could be the green Jell-O of years past, even as the ink is drying on the page. Eating and food writing has also become the arena for judging what and how others eat.

Reactions to concerns about what we should eat on the part of the affluent are often as strong as religious beliefs. On my computer screen, I see a picture of one of my favorite foods: a simple banana. But this one comes with a wicked smile and a warning: "Never eat these foods." Some foods have been declared sinful while others claim to save us, not from sin, but from grave conditions like cancer, diabetes, and heart attacks. You know the lists: "Eat these ten foods to avoid cancer." Or, "Eat these five foods to lose weight." The lists change frequently. Nathan Myhrvold, author of *The Art and Science of Bread*, claims that many of our ideas about what is bad for us are not based on scientific studies. While he excludes celiac disease from his comments about gluten, he says, "We have undergone what amounts to an attack of evil spirits: gluten will destroy your brain, it will give you cancer, it will kill you. We are the same people who talk to shamans" (Myhrvold 2014).

The media is full of exhortations to eat organically, seasonally, mindfully, raw, and locally. Although some of the trends have led to positive changes in how and what we eat, a frantic, frenetic concern about food is pervasive in the news; advertising caters to those who can afford to choose what and how to eat. Many of us love reading about food, the recipes, where to go not just for basic food, but good food, what's good for us, and what's in or out. Food writers write for those living with plenty and recommend which foods we should choose. I am guilty of greedily reading about food, always looking for the best recipe ever, the healthiest, or the easiest.

No wonder people gain and lose weight like yoyos. We are bombarded with mixed and ever-changing messages about food in our magazines and the media. In one magazine, I see, "Walk your way to two sizes smaller," and a few pages later, "Eat the best chocolate cake ever!" I prefer combining the two, "Walk your way over to the best chocolate cake ever,"—but I don't see that article! It's easy to indulge in both, eating bonbons while thinking about exercising. Both messages are on my plate with the burrito special of eggs and cheese and a sugar-free drink. I have seen people sprinkle in low-calorie sweeteners while adding cream to their coffee.

In the United States, the diet industry and weight-loss market swallow 40-80 billion dollars per year. In June 2011, the Boston Medical Center reported that 45 million Americans diet each year, many without success, and that an estimated 300 million people are dangerously overweight. Diets, like some foods, go in and then out of style. Reducing fats promised weight loss, followed by reducing carbs, and then eating low-calorie foods, with eliminating sugar as the latest trend. Recently, we are reading more about moderation in foods, including fats, sugars, and other carbohydrates.[2] We want to enjoy what we eat without worrying about gaining weight in

---

[2] (Groopman 2017, 92-97)

the spirit of the promises in our magazines and advertising. Costly diets claim cures for a wide variety of different ailments, promises of a successful life, or the assertion that having "a different body will result in a different life."[3]

It's not surprising that for many people, dieting is often associated with misery. As MFK Fisher writes, "The fine line between use and abuse cannot perhaps be clearer than in the human history of weight control. Writers from the beginning of time have listed the atrocities committed in the name of slenderness. Most of them, in one form or another, involve plain starvation. Most poor people, like most poor nations, are thin. In the US, we eat too much, and then we exaggerate our efforts to grow slim and well again."[4]

Some writers like Geneen Roth and Divya Gugnani, who struggled with dieting and unhappiness, discourage dieting as we've known it with its denial of fats, sugars, and carbohydrates. They suggest rethinking dieting or doing away with dieting as a means of losing weight (Roth 2010) (Gugnani 2011). In the book, *Sexy Women Eat: Secrets to Eating What You Want and Still Looking Fabulous*, Gugani writes about whipping her own and your *ass* into shape. When advising her readers not to indulge in soda pop, she asks, "Who wants an ass that could swallow up a thong anyway? Certainly not me."[5] The book is a sassy and often amusing read about various diets Gugani has tried. Many of her ideas, like portion control, seem sensible, though the book discourages certain foods — hardly "eating what you want and still looking fabulous" advice. Roth writes, "Women turn to food when they are not hungry because they are hungry for something they can't name: a connection to what is beyond the concerns of daily life. Something deathless, something sacred."[6] Even where there seems to be plenty of food, a deep hunger drives us. Everywhere we see discrepancies, advice, and obsessions about food. Physical hunger, obesity, and eating disorders are mingled together and not mutually exclusive in our culture.

Some zealous food concerns convey anxiety and emptiness. Being able to afford and choose what we eat does not keep us from being restless about food. A growling stomach is the sign of physical hunger. Extremes and rising discontent about how our food is raised indicates another concern. The food-obsessed, the overeater, and the troubled girl who suffers from anorexia reach to fill the emptiness with food or drastically deny it. Something is amiss. We are not satisfied. There is a sense of being spiritually adrift and bereft. Perhaps our souls are malnourished.

---

[3] (Roth 2010, 77)
[4] (Fisher 1961, 99-100
[5] (Gugnani 2011, 88)
[6] (Roth 2010, 32)

It's not all about the eating concerns of the wealthy. Writers cover the injustices of hunger too. An arresting question a few years ago caught my attention. The occasion was the USDA lowering the internal temperature requirements for commercially served pork from 160 to 145 degrees. "What does it say about America that medium-rare pork is bigger news than tens of thousands of North Africans that starved this year from a harsh mix of drought and war?"[7]

A narrow and limited focus on the temperature of pork, or eating food out of proportion to actual needs, are two examples of our outlook on food. But not everyone is concerned with such things. Many people don't spend time discussing whether they'll be eating natural or organic, or driving to where they'll get it, not only because of the expense. They scorn and distrust terms like organic, lite, whole grain, or quinoa, equating them with foo-foo food. Once home, they may not have the luxury of time or desire to experiment with food, or the ingredients on hand for trying different recipes. Many are busy, tired, working for minimum wage—and just relieved to have something—anything—to eat.

But that is not my situation. I come in the house hungry after jogging. My work is not physical, so I choose to exercise. I tell myself I've jogged, and I'm drawn to the left-over piece of chocolate cake or a scoop of ice cream. I blame it on the magazines. Exercise makes us hungry. I glance at the article about firming up the body by a little weight lifting only three times a week. It is time to make dinner.

I remember an interesting looking recipe for cooking chicken breasts and go look for it. But, before I can get to it, I see an article, "Get organized—lose pounds." What does organization have to do with it? Then I see one called, "Flatten your belly fast," from *Beauty and Body* and "40 all-new recipes" in the same issue. Oh, but I must check out what the "shortcake secrets" says, and then "the ten steps to save your heart." Then I see it: "The Ultimate Stuffed Chicken Breasts." Choosing or avoiding foods is on my mind as I walk to the refrigerator. What option will I choose? Something vegetarian, chicken breasts, or pork chops? Stuffed or svelte?

Sifting through the conflicting advice, I read and make some decisions about dinner that seem right today. Tomorrow, maybe not.

Like many people reading and writing about food, I both choose and worry that I will eat the wrong foods, adulterated foods, or take in too many calories while many humans have little choice, or don't have enough to eat. So, I choose, but uncomfortably. I worry about what my meal choices mean to those who are hungry and to the environment. I think about eating and food justice.

---

[7] (Levaux 2011, 30-31)

Should or can my plate have all these considerations piled on it like a balanced diet? These hand-wringing deliberations are some of the thought patterns that lead to thinking that food is dangerous, instead of a gift from God (Weaver-Zercher 2013). I was raised on Jesus' words about worry in Matthew 6:25: "Do not worry about your life, what you will eat or drink."

I prepare our dinner of a simple romaine salad with tomatoes and brown rice. But even then I can't silence the questions: Were they sprayed with pesticides and perhaps genetically modified? Were the chicken breasts pumped up with antibiotics? The brown rice perhaps now laced with some arsenic? If we're still hungry after that (and maybe if I'm not) I will have a small bowl of low-fat ice cream even though the refined sugar or corn syrup adds calories without adding nutrition, but then there is the calcium. I will have a dark chocolate and a glass of Merlot. After all, aren't they good for our hearts?

Chicken Marsala with Sage

Makes 4 servings

4 thin skinless and boneless chicken breast halves,
(each halved horizontally)
All-purpose flour
6 tablespoons butter
1 tablespoon. chopped fresh sage
1 cup imported dry Marsala
1 cup canned low-salt chicken broth
Fresh sage leaves

1. Sprinkle chicken with salt and pepper. Dust with flour; shake off excess.
2. Melt 3 tablespoons butter in large skillet over medium-high heat. Add chicken with chopped sage.
3. Sauté until brown and cooked through, about 3 minutes per side and a bit more for thicker pieces.
4. Transfer chicken to a platter (but return the skillet to the stove).
5. Tent chicken with foil.
6. Add Marsala and broth to the skillet; bring to a boil, scraping up any browned bits. Boil until sauce is reduced to ½ cup, about 10 minutes.
7. Season with salt and pepper; spoon over chicken. Garnish with sage leaves.

This is wickedly easy and good, thanks to the butter. Follow it with a piece of dark chocolate.

Morning comes, and we are hungry. I am thinking about food and meals again. While my husband Clay was still having breakfast, I asked him what he'd like me to pack him for lunch. Usually, if he does not have a luncheon work meeting, he agrees to the lunch. But this day he laughed and said, "The language you speak is the language of food."

What is that language?

In the last few pages, I wrote about jogging and coming home hungry, and thought about all the talk about food in the media. We see the pictures of food flashing on advertisements and hear advice about what we should eat and what we should avoid. Is this the language of food? Magazines and television are larded up with a language of food. We use foody words to describe life's conditions of one kind or another: we rub *salt* in the wounds, say the story was *spicy*, note that fear was *eating* him up or that he's sweet as *honey,* or the *apple* of her eye, and ask, isn't it the *berries?* Are these words of eating the language of food?

I'm surrounded by food language. I write grocery lists noting what I need and will prepare for meals. Shopping for food and then preparing it takes time—more time than we spend eating it.

Perhaps the best way for me to describe the language of food is a hunger for abundance—not a consuming greed for more but an appetite for the sweetness of life and a taste for the goodness of the world. (Capon 1967) My language begins with memories at a table in the Northwest with my parents and siblings. We are asking for a blessing for daily food. The Lord's Prayer, "Give us this day our daily bread," a habit so natural, the murmuring before dinner. Later I realized how profound this simple prayer is. That short time with eyes closed opened a world beyond our mundane concerns almost like a time-out calling us to leave behind what was and begin anew. As a child, while I was thinking that the food would be cold if the prayer went on too long, my parents understood the petition "Give us this day our daily bread" as a reminder that we are in need and not so independent. We depend on others for our food; we depend on the weather for our crops. The prayer is not limited to my wants and desires, but a prayer reminding us that we are in a community (*our* daily bread), and that we are hungry and human.

Mom or Dad read the Bible to us after the meal. The biblical imagery and metaphors of plants, trees, food, and nature speak of need and hunger while promising a fullness or abundance for all. The biblical invitations to banquets, feasts, and food are inclusive and seem to invite both those who have plenty and those who are poor. "Listen, listen to me, and eat what is good, and you will delight in the richest of fare," says Isaiah 55:2. The language of restoration is food: "They will plant vineyards and drink their wine; they will make gardens and eat their fruit," says Amos 9:14. "He has filled the hungry with good things," notes Luke 1:53a.

Abundance is often defined in culture in terms of possessions, success, popularity, and power—whatever makes us comfortable. Jesus seems less concerned about our eating lavish dinners or large quantities of expensive food and more concerned about our limited desires. He invites us to imagine more. Wealthy or poor, we are easily satisfied with what brings comfort and what we are in the habit of doing, not the freedom and joy that makes our lives large and satisfying. The Bible invites abandoning what binds, limits, and keeps us from the abundant life. Instead of nibbling at the scraps, imagine being hungry for what matters and seeking the food which nourishes us.

C.S. Lewis captures this idea well when he writes: "We are half-hearted creatures, fooling about with drink and sex and ambition when infinite joy is offered us, like an ignorant child who wants to go on making mud pies in a slum because he cannot imagine what is meant by the offer of a holiday at the sea. We are far too easily pleased." [8]

Like many neighbors and relatives, my parents had a large garden with a variety of vegetables. A row of dahlias in all colors and sizes graced one border of the garden beside the road, but it was mostly rows of lettuce, radishes, potatoes, and corn that filled the space. We buttered homemade bread when we came home from school. We tasted life around a table in a large kitchen where we ate dinners with meat, potatoes, often two vegetables, fresh milk, and the fish Dad caught. I was short-sighted; I thought everyone ate like we did. My parents reminded my sisters and me to finish what was on our plates by telling us about children in other countries who didn't have enough. But I had no complaints about the food.

Even so, I did not think of the small dairy farm where I was raised as a place of abundance. My parents worked at other jobs and would have liked more financial security. The work was hard and dirty. I look back without nostalgia at feeding calves and bucking bales during haying season, and my parents' hard work. I sometimes grumbled about my evening chores on the farm after working all day picking berries or beans for local growers in the summer. It didn't matter that we lived in a strong dairy community and neighboring farmers were doing similar work. I wanted to do other things. Abundance is more than farm-fresh food on the table.

People who are attracted to farming have often not lived on one. True farmers are independent and passionate about the work but realistic. Many were raised on farms and prepared by the hard work of their parents. Those who romanticize farming tend to live in cities.

Some think of farms where I grew up as idyllic, but one cannot make a living on small farms anymore. That change occurred some time ago. As I recently read in an article about industrial farming, "We may think of rural America as a halcyon pastoral of red barns and the Waltons, but today it's also a land of unemployment,

---

[8] (Lewis 1988, 362)

poverty, despair, and methamphetamines."[9]

When Clay and I were married, going to college, and living two thousand miles from our parents, I made meals some of which were based on Mom's and Grandma's recipes, scaled down. Mom had often made not one vegetable for our meals but two. We were penny-pinching, and one was enough for Clay and me.

Still, I had learned something about abundance at my parents' table. As Joy Harjo writes, "the world begins (and ends) at a kitchen table. No matter what, we must eat to live."[10] While helping prepare food, and while cooking and eating, I experienced love, arguing, joking, laughter, stories, Bible reading, prayer, and sometimes tears—the full gamut of life. It was at the table that I became hungry for more. Food is the language the body craves and hunger the language of the soul.

The memorable 1987 film *Babette's Feast* portrays both hunger of the body and of the soul for something better and heavenly. Babette has been hired to cook and clean for two adult sisters who live modestly with their father, a pastor in a small village. Babette changes their lives and their small community by using an unexpected fortune to make a sumptuous feast for the sisters and their community. The contrast of the beginning scenes of the simple soups they are eating, followed by the preparation of the feast with its specialties, is stunning. Babette has all kinds of delicacies delivered. Once the feast is on the table, the sisters and guests begin eating with their usual pious solemnity, but when they taste the delicious foods, they break into smiles. The language of food changes their lives.

Watching that story unfold, I was reminded of the story of Mary lavishly pouring out expensive perfume on Jesus' feet, the parable of the banquet when those who likely can't reciprocate but need a feast come to the banquet, and the account of Jesus at a wedding, turning the water into wine.

The Bible is full of accounts of Jesus eating, of feasting, and of banquets, all inviting us to live expansively. We, whose stomachs are never full for long, are empty, hungry, and waiting for a place at the table. We are satisfied with too little if we are not pursuing the abundance of life, hungry as wolves. If we are sated, we grow dull. Hunger keeps us moving, aware of our needs, aware that we are starving for something better.

In this book, I speak what my husband Clay earlier called the language of food. I write about cooking and eating, accidents, laughter, serving food, waiting on tables, opinions, trends in food practices, blessings, and meals and experiences in several countries. I invite you to see what it is like at my table. I invite you to be like Erica Jong, who has ignored the raspberries in her driveway and one day recognizes their beauty and tastes their

---

[9] (Kristof 2014)
[10] (Harjo 1994)

glory, to "imagine what wonders lie in store for [you]!"[11] As Harjo's poem about our lives around kitchen tables says, "We must eat to live." Let's dine hungrily, laughing and living abundantly.

Crêpes Maison

16 ounces softened cream cheese
Zest of 1 lemon
2 tablespoons lemon juice
½ cup of sugar plus ¼ cup
1 tablespoon cornstarch
2 pints of raspberries, divided

1. Mix the cream cheese, lemon zest, and sugar. Add the lemon juice.
2. Gently add the mixture to the crêpes. Depending on the size of the crêpe, I usually have about a dozen.
3. Roll them up and place in a 13x9 pan.
4. Crush one pint and a half of berries and put through a sieve. Don't worry if there are a few seeds left. Place them in a pan with 1/4 cup of sugar mixed with the cornstarch.
5. Heat the mixture over medium heat until slightly thickened.
6. Pour over crêpes and bake at 350 degrees for 30 minutes. Before serving, sprinkle some fresh raspberries on top.
Note: There are many recipes for crêpes. I find they work best if made in a small cast iron skillet.

Prayer: Lord, help us see the disparities between our greed and those who are hungry. Forgive obsessions that keep us from enjoying food and for our ideas of scarcity and the limitations of our pursuits. Teach us to discern how we should eat, so others have food, our earth is sustained, and we stay in good health. Open our eyes to fullness and joy.

---

[11] (Jong 1991)

2

Playing with Food: Smearing, Foaming, Loafing, and Lab-Grown (Groan)

They'd been working on the scallop dish for weeks. It was a thing of beauty: a smear of black nori puree on the bottom of the bowl; then a layer of sea scallops and chanterelles and possibly clams; and then, spooned on top in front of the customer, a soft heap of foaming dashi (kelp and dried-bonito broth), made intentionally unstable with just a little methylcellulose, so that in front of the customer's eyes the bubbles would burst and dissipate into a fishy liquid, at exactly the speed that foam from a wave dissipates onto sand. It looked like the sea and tasted like the sea, and Chang was extremely proud of it.[12]

Bon appetit? I tried reading this description again when I was hungry, and it didn't appeal to me any more than the first time I read it. Chang, aka the chef on the edge, uses odd ingredients in his new restaurant, called Ko and described as "adventurous." In a world in which it is hard for some to find or pay for food, it is disconcerting

---

[12] (MacFarquhar 2008, 58)

to read about the opposite end of the food spectrum, where rich tongues eat expensive and weird fare.

Eating has been referred to as a sport, and thanks to all the posting and sharing, it has become a spectator sport (Fauchald 2011). There must be some pressure on the part of chefs to surprise and dramatize food for those for whom eating has become more like a recreation than a basic need, where culinary pleasure has taken a turn to the competitive and extreme. Still, I can't imagine that anyone would do well for long with Chang's scallop dish. Given a choice, a child would likely choose to eat Cheerios and prefer to play with Chang's dish at the beach. Even Chang eats noodles and goes out for pizza. But still, I had to love him when the article said he "reveres" the molecular cook and chef named Ferran Adrià who originated the foam craze and "rethinks" food. "Poetic," and "abstract" are terms that describe his food, and, of course, he shares my name. Our names and a love of cooking and eating may be all that Adria and I have in common. His terms for food—"deconstructivist," "poetic" and "abstract" —make me realize that the extent of the art in my cooking is the sprinkling of paprika on potato salad or carving a watermelon into the shape of a basket.

When I read about Adrià, I imagine chefs doing everything they can to get people to pay attention to their provocative and dramatic food as though it's not really food but art we're eating. I once asked a manager at an ice cream store whether any of the ice cream flavors had not sold well and had had to be removed from the shelf. All of the many flavors of ice cream had sold well except mushroom crunch ice cream. We need creative chefs, but mushroom crunch ice cream? A New York Times article (Bruni, Dinner and Derangement 2011) tells of a restaurant trying too hard to be stylish and serving flavored waters between their eleven courses. (One was leek and radish; another was jasmine and seaweed.) Although a flair for style and delicious food can co-exist, they are hardly the same thing.

Food creativity may be overdone, but experiments like those of Chang and Adrià may also lead to ways of providing tastier and healthier food and feeding our planet more effectively using plant-based food and even pseudo meat like lab-grown shmeat.

On May 20, 2008, Ketzel Levine reported on National Public Radio that though tissue-cultured meat had been the subject of science fiction, now it is being grown in labs "from Norway to North Carolina," and produced in the same way that skin patches are grown in solutions of nutrients. Tissue-cultured meat has the advantage of creating actual meat without killing animals. Winston Churchill proposed it as early as 1932. In his essay, "Fifty Years Hence" he wrote, "We shall escape the absurdity of growing a whole chicken in order to eat the breast or wing, by growing these parts separately under a suitable medium." Vladimir Mironov, a biologist, is working on producing tissue-cultured meat in which he turns formless, textureless patches of the stuff into mass-produced meat sheets called shmeat.

Naysayers include the molecular biologist Margaret Mellon from the Union of Concerned Scientists who believes that factory grown meat kept at constant temperatures and keeping all those cells sterile would require tremendous energy and fossil fuel. The whole idea seems not very appealing or appetizing even to people who don't worry very much about where their meat comes from (Levine 2008) or how it is produced. Yet to be fair, I have picked up a wing or leg of a chicken and found that thinking about where it comes from and how it gets to my plate makes my appetite disappear. Some vegans' criterion is if they can't look an animal in the eye, they don't eat it.

But lower-tech food solutions that do not require huge amounts of energy already exist in the market and don't require looking into an eye before biting into them. A bit of tinkering and imagination has already given us the Boca Burger, although the missing meat, in this case, has been replaced by processed soy and corn products and some ingredients I don't recognize. I make my own veggie burgers, one using old-fashioned oats and the other garbanzo or black beans. Once they are formed into patties and baked or fried, and slipped into a bun with onions, relish (without high fructose), catsup, and mustard, they are more delicious than many hamburgers. In his article entitled "Fake Chicken," Mark Bittman writes that if vegetable products can taste more like the real thing, why wouldn't we eat them? We'd avoid killing so many animals, eat less meat, which is healthier, avoid bacteria, and reduce animal waste and the ingestion of antibiotics given to animals (Bittman 2012).

In the prisons where I worked for decades, substitutes for meat were often extra helpings of peanut butter. But even in prison, there was room for creativity. The food the prisoners ate varied, depending on how the cooks used the ingredients. Most of the time the food appeared fine-looking and colorful, though not fixed with the flair of a Chang or Ferran, nor particularly creative or well spiced. But then the prisons I worked in served food under the auspices of dieticians who were mandated to ensure prisoners received the requisite amounts of protein and carbohydrates. The challenge was to make meals as attractive as possible for a large group with varied tastes.

I recently tuned in to a TV program on food served in prison. The program showed prisoners making creative spreads, meals, and desserts from goods they purchased at prison stores. When I worked in the Michigan prisons, prisoners who could afford it, ate snacks and meals from the prison stores. Some ate these store foods in the place of the meals provided, while others ate the food to supplement their regular prison meals. That's understandable: prisoners grow tired of institutional food and crave snacks just as many people do on the outside.

When the prisoners in the TV program were interviewed, not only did all but one of the prisoners interviewed have nothing positive to say about the prison food, they also all complained about not getting enough. Some had stolen food from the kitchen. One prisoner proudly showed how he had stuffed a bagful of food down the front of his pants.

When prisoners abuse or misuse food (throwing it at employees is considered "misuse") or become "creative" in other ways like food fights, they can be placed on "food loaf" —a punishment approved by the American Correctional standards—usually for a short time. "The loaf" continues to be controversial, but although unpleasant, it contains all the nutrition of what the rest of the prison population is eating. All the meat, potatoes, and vegetables are included, but they are blended and processed together. The whole meal is then shaped into a loaf, but according to prisoners, it's not your mother's or father's meatloaf. The media often do not understand this. One newspaper writer who had likely never had a prisoner hit him with food, discussed the loaf as though it were fed routinely to prisoners and not a consequence of their abuse of food, and described it as "a disgusting pressed amalgam of pulverized food."[13] But the punishment works. After one helping of food loaf, most prisoners are very sorry that they tossed their tomato on the floor or threw their beans at Officer Newhouse and beg to come off the loaf.

On the TV program mentioned earlier, a prison employee made a loaf consisting of cabbage, ground beef, and a grain, among some other foods. The employee as well as the reporter did not think the nutraloaf, as it was called, tasted too bad, though the prisoners disagreed. One man said he wouldn't feed it to his dog.

In fact, the prison loaf may be more nutritious than the grocery stores' and fast-food restaurants' nuggets or patties or loaves that taste like meat but don't even have meat or even shmeat in them. They look somewhat like food loaf but are often lab-grown and include vegetables modified with chemicals and gristle.

Perhaps we lack art and imagination. Perhaps we can learn to enjoy cruelty-free foods. Or perhaps we never will face the harm we are doing by our carnivorous diets.

I think of Art Carney on the old television comedy, "The Honeymooners" with Jackie Gleason. Times were tough, and when Jack and Art came home one night without paychecks, there was no steak, only celery sticks. They sat in their kitchen chairs looking glum. Jack told Art to imagine it was steak. Art couldn't leave it alone. He munched on his celery mmm, ahh, such good steak, until Gleason roared for him to "shut up." The celery may be in some of our plant-based burgers posing as beef, in the freezer meat department. If it tastes like meat and smells like meat, eat it up, and if it doesn't, with a little ketchup and mustard, it soon may. As many have written, "Ladies and gentlemen start your grills" to get that fired flavor whether for meats or for vegetables.

---

[13] (Sorkin 2013, 32-35)

While prisoners who abuse food must eat the food loaf, others of us are often confronted with and sometimes captivated by tinkered-with, stylized faux food that is cheap, full of chemicals, and readily available. We are prisoners of the market—unless we free ourselves to grow food and create ways of cooking that go beyond temporary trends, whether mushroom crunch ice cream or food full of air foaming on our plates.

The following recipes are simple, delicious, and satisfying even to most carnivores. Feel free to experiment by using different herbs, and even other vegetables, like grated carrot or chopped celery, as additions or substitutes for the ones listed.

Garbanzo Burgers

1 15-oz can of garbanzo beans, drained and rinsed
1⅓ cup rolled oats
1 cup water
½ onion, chopped
¼ cup drained and chopped frozen artichoke hearts, thawed
¼ teaspoon ground cumin
1 clove garlic, minced
¼ teaspoon cayenne pepper or paprika
1½ tablespoons soy sauce
1 to 2 tablespoons olive oil
6 whole wheat buns

1. Wash and drain beans and then place them in a food processor and run on low until beans are crumbly like ground meat.
2. Transfer to a large mixing bowl and add the remaining ingredients, except the olive oil.
3. Combine and let sit for 10-15 minutes, until all the water is absorbed. The mixture will be rather mushy.
4. Shape patties by scooping ½ cup and laying out on a piece of waxed paper. Make 6 large patties. Pat each patty down slightly to shape.
5. In a large skillet, heat the oil over medium-high heat. Using a spatula, carefully lift patties off the waxed paper and onto the skillet.
6. Cook on both sides until golden brown. Serve on bread buns with burger condiments of your choice, such as ketchup, mustard, lettuce, red onion, and sliced tomatoes. Makes 6 burgers.

Food: An Appetite for Life

Rolled Oat Burgers

2 cups water
2 cups old-fashioned rolled oats or GF oats
2 tablespoons tamari or soy sauce
1 tablespoons plus 2 teaspoons pure olive oil
1 cup diced onions
½ cup grated carrots
½ cup diced celery
½ cup diced red bell peppers
2 cloves garlic, minced
2 teaspoons dried oregano
Fresh basil—6 leaves minced, or one teaspoon dried
½ teaspoon fresh ground black pepper

1. Bring water to a boil in a saucepan over medium-high heat. Add oats, tamari or soy sauce and 1 tablespoon oil.
2. Reduce heat to low and cook 2 minutes; remove from heat and set aside.
3. In a skillet, heat the remaining oil over medium heat. Add rest of ingredients and sauté 2 minutes or until vegetables are softened.
4. Add to cooked oat mixture and combine well. Chill at least 2 hours or overnight.
5. Preheat oven to 375 degrees. Using an ice cream scoop, or ¼ cup measure, form each portion into a ball and flatten slightly.
6. Place on a lightly oiled baking sheet and bake 20 minutes until golden brown. Makes 16 patties.

Nutrition per burger: 97 calories, 0 mg cholesterol, 3g fat, 80mg sodium, 4g protein, 15g carbohydrate.

For Veggie Loaf

1. Mix the ingredients and instead of measuring out ¼ cups for patties, place the oatmeal/vegetable mixture in a loaf pan and form a loaf. (One egg can be added for a moister mixture.)
2. Mix up ¼ cup of catsup and 2 teaspoons of mustard, and a little brown sugar if you like, and smooth it over the top of the loaf.
3. Bake at 350 degrees for about an hour.

Prayer:
Lord, we enjoy the creativity of chefs and good cooks. Keep us from following foolish food practices and food charlatans and help us use our creativity to feed people without abusing our earth.

3

Foragers

"Since Eve ate apples, much depends on dinner."
—Lord Byron

Foraging for food is a hot movement and Rene Redzepi, the foraging chef, exemplifies how successful it can be. Food media rave about Noma in Copenhagen "the best restaurant in the world," where Redzepi is the chef (Kramer 2011) (Muhlke 2012). Foraging is a backlash. Instead of going to supermarkets with so many products that it can be difficult to choose from among them, some people are finding tasty treasures without having had a hand in planting them. The quality of our industrialized food has chefs foraging for what's wild, seasonal, and local. Redzepi calls it "treasure hunting," claiming he "got connected to the sea and soil, and now they're an integral part of him. I experience the world through food," he says.[14]

---

[14] (Kramer 2011, 89)

For the novice, foraging can be tricky. Mushrooms grow in the foothills of the mountains here in the Northwest, but without an expert along to identify them, or making a habit of using reliable mushroom identification guides, people do consume poisonous varieties, sometimes with a fatal outcome. Redzepi studies botany to determine what is poisonous and safe to eat.

The most adventuresome foraging I've undertaken on my own is picking the blackberries which grow prolifically along the ditches in northwest Washington State. When someone from the Midwest asked me about "planting" blackberries, I laughed. In the Northwest, you must be careful that a thicket of them does not spring up so quickly in your driveway that you are unable to get your car into the garage. Recently, I read about eating burning or stinging nettles, which also grow along the ditches here. Apparently cooking destroys the part of the plant that stings, leaving a plate of vitamin-packed spinach-like greens. (Check out recipes on-line.) Fresh food that grows wild that we didn't plant and is available for the taking is a kind of free lunch. But foraging is for the cautious. Two of my sisters learned the hard way that foraging is not to be taken lightly, as I explain later.

Good food is available, and people all over the world forage to supplement their diets. Animals, unless they are domesticated, have learned what will sustain them. Seagulls scavenge what the tides leave on shore. The deer crossing my path in the morning munch on plants in someone's yard or the golf course grass—the ways of the wild transported to suburbia. I hope we leave something besides our garbage that they can glean. I draw the line at allowing bugs to forage in my house.

Some time ago ants marched so sneakily into my kitchen they'd appear on my cupboard or often the kitchen sink without any indication of where they had come from or where they were going! Not long trails of them following a leader, but three or four randomly arriving between 8 and 9 AM, though they arrived at other times too. I'm sure they were in this together though. Quoted in "Kin and Kind" by Jonah Lehrer,[15] E.O. Wilson, who has studied ants extensively, claims that their "biological success is especially remarkable because it depends entirely on their ability to cooperate, to form intricate societies structured around hard work and shared sacrifice." Jonah Lehrer cites the Proverbs 6:6 passage, "Go to the ant, thou sluggard; consider her ways and be wise."

Sometimes these kitchen ants would seem to stand up and sniff the breeze for an enemy or more likely a crumb I'd left on the counter. Regardless of their sophisticated societies, I was in no mood to consider their ways. I wasn't sure what they were looking for, but I became obsessive about food—covering it and leaving no traces of it on the countertops. I knew I was watching the foragers too much. I told myself I was looking for

---

[15] (Lehrer. 2012, 36-42)

their home or ant hill, not wasting my time like the sluggard told to "go to the ant."

They were not the smallest I've ever seen or the largest—fortunately, although they grew very large in my mind. And I preferred them to the mealy bugs that I once took home from the grocery store, which were sneakier since they found their way to almost any grain or flour in my cupboards until they flew out as moths. Since I have different types of flours and meal for the bread I make in the bread maker, the destruction was great. Now, I refrigerate or freeze all my grains. At least ants are out in the open, and not hiding their vermin and larvae or reproducing in the flour canister.

Fortunately, they stayed on one side of the kitchen until I left a few baking chocolate bars on the counter overnight. I caught one walking around the package. Chocolate-covered ants?

At first, I wasn't worried. I've read about many completely organic and healthy deterrents so poisons that might affect humans wouldn't be necessary. I went online and saw all the things ants detest. Borax especially and baby powder were supposedly very offensive. Acids too, like orange, lemon, and vinegar would send them scurrying away. I went with Borax, which I sprinkled on the backs of the counters. But the ants were persistent and not to be deterred. They avoided the Borax, and while they sometimes looked sickly and died in the sink, they were still THERE! Next, leaving the Borax on the back of the counters, I filled a spray bottle with part water and part vinegar. At first, I sprayed it around and wiped it up. That was fine with the ants. Then, I sprayed the mixture on the counter and just left it—several times a day. It helped. And then one day three ants at one time were on the counter.

While I had breakfast, a piece of my hair fell out of place on my face, and I panicked certain it was an ant falling from my head going after my oatmeal or the sugar in it. Later I had an itch, and madly slapped a small black piece of lint on my arm that I swore was moving. One morning while reading at the table when it was quiet, I imagined I heard some munching and rustling near my cupboard. I woke up one morning with a small hive on my skin close to my eye. I was convinced it was the fault of one of the ant invaders. They grew a couple of sizes larger in my dreams.

They had to go, less for the health risk they posed than for my mental stability.

I broke down and bought poison—one with a floral scent, for me, not the ants. I sprayed the outside doors and windows—especially the door that was cracking at the bottom and in need of replacement and where the ants may have come in. Fewer ants came in, but they still arrived. Next, I sprayed under the sink, the first spray inside the house. I still used the vinegar treatment too.

I never did find out what they liked except perhaps chocolate. Some are attracted to sweets and others, apparently, to grease. I won't say they finally got the message, but they left after one sick-looking, slow-moving ant died on my kitchen floor. As much as I'd love to love nature, I can't bring myself to co-exist with bug beings in the house, and when it happens, only drastic measures will do. I'm cautiously optimistic. I've won this battle, but have I won the war?

Rene Redzepi, the human forager, says something about ants too. "Digging into soil, we found large ants that tasted like a wonderful, exciting blend of lemongrass, ginger, and lovage. Entomophagy—eating insects as food—might prove that our pale, Protestant nation can be spicy after all. Insects, beware!"[16] Who knew? Why was I using poison when I could have sprinkled them on my cereal like raisins?

After all, we eat bugs unintentionally. Laura Drouillard reports that "Title 21, Part 110.110 of the Code of Federal Regulations allows the Food and Drug Administration (FDA) to establish maximum levels of natural or unavoidable defects in foods for human use said to present no health hazard. The booklet, 'The Food Defect Action Levels: Levels of Natural or Unavoidable Defects in Foods That Present No Health Hazards for Humans,' lists how much of these naturally occurring defects are allowed before the government intervenes." Rodent hairs are allowed—in small increments. "Which is Greater" a quiz asks, "the number of head coaches in the University of Michigan's football program history or the amount of rodent hairs permissible per 50 grams of ground cinnamon?" The answer to this one is the number of head coaches—eighteen, while the FDA will step in if there are eleven or more rodent hairs per 50 grams of ground cinnamon.[17]

I've read recipes for wax worm cookies, fried green tomato hornworms, and the nutritional value of grasshoppers (Booth 2014) (Tarre 2014).

Most of us may not be ready to forage for food and especially not bugs, though Redzepi's ideas about eating what's seasonal and local may have advantages. My mom called the Pacific Northwest the land of milk and honey, although the honey, as I mention elsewhere, likely referred to Dad, who drew her like a bear going after honey. I could live on salmon (less available as we overfish) and berries, but in the winter, if we ate seasonal and local, we'd be eating what was stored, frozen, canned, dried, or grown in greenhouses, as people have in the past. The savings of not transporting food in and out of regions may be a plus. But some people have suggested that transportation costs can be more economical if growing something locally requires more resources than growing it farther away.

A forager chef is now preparing food at Lummi Island, one of my favorite places. Unlike islands in the area, like Orcas or San Juan in Puget Sound, Lummi has not been developed into a tourist destination. It is close

---

[16] (Muhlke 2012, 74)
[17] (Drouillard 2012, 61)

to the mainland. The Whatcom Chief ferry carries cars and passengers to their destination in five minutes. To get to our property, we turn left from the ferry, go by a modest general store, the Islander, one of a few commercial properties on the island, and turn left again on Seacrest. Proceed a few miles and turn left into our drive. Through the Douglas firs and cedars, we see the waters of Hale Passage below, and Bellingham Bay to the east and the iconic peak of Mt. Baker beyond that, breathtakingly beautiful.

Until recently, Lummi Island was not a destination for food. Then Blaine Wetzel became the new chef at the Willows Inn. Wetzel is young, but he has the distinction of having cooked at Copenhagen's Noma where Rene Redzepi was the chef. Wetzel has attracted people who are serious about food and garnered the media's attention for the restaurant (Clement 2011). Part of the attraction is that every ingredient is sourced within a few miles of the Willows Inn (Dickerman 2013). We made plans to go, though we knew it would be an expensive evening. I kept the menu of snacks and dinner items served on the evening of our meal, many of them foraged from the beaches.

I remember the exquisite tastes of small bites not unlike a tasting menu I experienced in the Netherlands. (See "Taking a Nibble without a Quibble," next chapter.) If we liked something, well, it was about small portions and tasting, and that plate was whisked away. I am a proletariat. One of my favorite dishes that evening was plentiful hearty bread with pan drippings without a whiff of the Pacific Ocean or a hint that it had been foraged on the shore.

If we had to forage, we would be taking lessons from Redzepi, who has made himself familiar with the wild things he's foraging, so he doesn't consume something poisonous, or we'd be learning from the animals as MFK Fisher tells us, describing foraging and how they survive without taking our advice (Fisher 1961, 5). I mentioned earlier picking blackberries, the only foraging in which I've engaged. I have two sisters who did a little foraging on our parents' small farm. They were thinking like Eve in the Garden of Eden: if it looks good, it must be good to eat. The story about the part if-it-looks-too-good-to-be-true-it-probably-is, had not yet sunk in.

My sister Ruth ate the beautiful yellow skunk cabbage *Lysichiton Americanus* that grew in the swamp on my parent's farm. I don't know why. Part of the arum family, the plant has a "skunky" odor so she can't have been enticed by its smell. Not only did she eat some of the plants, she then disappeared, as if she had eaten of the fruit and been expelled from our garden before she could tempt us or anyone else with it. A frantic search by my mother and father was fruitful. She had a way of falling asleep sometimes when she played and had fallen asleep in the car in our garage where my parents later found her sawing away. Skunk cabbage, considered a weed, can be used for food if cooked properly. But, raw, it can seriously irritate the mouth and eaten in large quantities, it is poisonous. She lived to tell about it.

Another sister ate some of the pods of a tree in our yard by the driveway, likely a golden chain, *Laburnum watereri*. Both the blossoms and the pods are considered very poisonous. By the time my parents rushed her to the doctor, my sister was pale and limp. Her stomach was pumped out; the eating of that tree was a serious matter. Foraging is not for amateurs.

I understand the attraction to flowers. Roses are beautiful and elegant, and I can't think of a more intoxicating, sweet-smelling flower. They are related to the strawberry (part of the Rosaceous family). Many varieties of roses grew at Francis Park in Lansing, Michigan, close to where I lived, and I could scarcely take in enough of their essence simply by smelling them. I wanted to inhale them so that smell would stay with me longer than one whiff gave me, even though I had to dodge the bees tucked in their petals. We hunger for the permanence of smells like that. When I lived in Vancouver B.C. for a summer, I wandered into a small grocery store looking for flowers. In the back, I saw some white fragrant Asian lilies. The clerk approached me and, anticipating my question, said, "No, they are for odor." She was practical. They were also pleasing to the eye. A child may have been tempted to take a bite from those white beauties.

While it is tempting to eat what looks good, which is why we often place bright-colored foods on our plates, what is pleasing to the eye or the nose may be poisonous if consumed. In contrast, some green vegetables are not going to win any food contests for looks. If the snake had offered Eve broccoli instead of an apple or some other type of juicy fruit, would she have given in to temptation?

Perhaps Eve would have eaten the broccoli because she was told that on eating it, she'd have wisdom, just as our advertisements promise us new life if we eat some super food like broccoli or kale. In the Genesis story, we are told that "the woman saw that the fruit of the tree was good for *food* and *pleasing to the eye*, and also desirable for gaining *wisdom*."

Once expelled from the Garden and forever after, food was "domesticated." Food was planted, grown, harvested, and eaten "by the sweat of our brows" with weeds and thistles always threatening it. Once we've tasted the fruit someone else planted and harvested and brought to the supermarkets, it's hard to go back to living innocently, and foraging for food, especially in urban areas. Eve stepped back from foraging when she was offered not an easy Eden but a hard world of toil, civilization, and dependence on one another for food. Farming and the knowledge it takes was her new life.

Food binds us together. Farming frees most of us to live without tilling the soil or hunting for food. Redzepi has the luxury of supplementing what he forages with mussels from fishermen and vegetables grown by farmers in cultivated gardens.

It behooves us to be knowledgeable about what we eat and what is available at our feet. We need wisdom connecting us to what and how we eat: children need to know that food doesn't grow in expensive packaging. Eating what is local and seasonal seems wise, but since we can't go back to Eden, cultivated farms will feed the world we have.

Apples of Eve

2 tablespoons butter
2 large apples, such as Winesap or Granny Smith, peeled, cored, and sliced
¼ cup packed brown sugar
Dash of cinnamon
2 ounces rum, opt.
½ pint vanilla ice cream

1. In medium skillet, heat butter until melted. Add apples and sauté, stirring a few minutes.
2. Add brown sugar and cinnamon, stirring until brown sugar dissolves. Cook, stirring until sauce becomes thick and syrupy.
3. Heat rum in small saucepan.
4. Ignite with match and pour flaming into sauce.
5. Spoon flaming sauce over ice cream in dessert dishes. Makes 2 servings.

Note: This dessert provides sweet comfort in place of the wisdom I will never have.
If you have a bit more time, the following apple dessert is also delicious and doesn't require a pan.

Apple Crostata

Crust

Pastry for one-crust 9-inch pie. The following is a basic recipe:

1½ cups all-purpose flour
2 tablespoons sugar
1 stick chilled unsalted butter, cut into pieces
3 tablespoons ice water

Filling

4-5 cups of peeled, sliced apples
½ teaspoon cinnamon
½ cup brown sugar

1. Combine flour and sugar in a food processor; pulse to combine the butter, until the mixture looks like coarse meal. Add the water and process until the pastry clumps.
2. Add more water in small amounts if the mixture seems dry. Shape the dough into a disk and refrigerate it for one hour.
3. Roll out the dough to an 11-inch round. Place on a cookie sheet. If you wish, you can line a 9-inch tart pan with the pastry or make it into a crostata (instructions follow in step 4).
4. Mix the apples, cinnamon, and sugar and place them in the middle of the pastry on the cookie sheet, leaving a 2-inch border. Fold the pastry up on the apples, pinching the edge. Bake at 375 degrees for about an hour until the apples are tender and the crust is browned.

Eating Raw

Eating unadulterated, natural food is undoubtedly part of the attraction of foraging. Related to foraging is the trend of eating food raw. Like foraging, eating raw, except for meat, suggests something wholesome and healthy. A documentary film called "Food Patriots," about people planting gardens and growing their food in urban as well as rural areas, shows them digging up carrots and other vegetables and eating them raw, right out of the garden. Documentaries about food are helping spread the message that fresh organic food can be eaten raw.

Several years ago, I loaded my old sewing machine, which I had not been using, into my car to deliver it to a stay-at-home mom who would. She was cheerful, and when she saw me looking at the jars and pots on open shelves in her porch before entering the kitchen, she left off talking about how she'd use the sewing machine. She could barely contain her enthusiasm about raw foods and the community with whom she exchanged recipes and prepared meals. Some of the recipes seemed labor intensive, but then she did not claim that eating raw was easier than cooking food.

I am relieved to read that a raw food diet is not essential to good health, though including raw foods is a good thing. Phew. Munching on a carrot from the garden or refrigerator is one thing, but who can resist, especially on a chilly day, a stew, a steaming plate of roasted potatoes, roast beef, scrambled eggs, a dessert of Apples of Eve flambé? Advocates will make the case for a raw foods diet, but I will leave that to them. As long as I have a fire, a stove, or a grill, I will cook as well as graze. And one could ask, what is considered a "raw" food? Even uncooked foods can't always be considered raw as I write in "Milky Way."

Prayer:
Lord, thank you for the abundance of our earth and the food available under our feet, on the trees, and in our seas, and the tools for agriculture.

A Nibble without a Quibble

"Appetizers are those little bits you eat until you lose your appetite."
—Anonymous

The Lazy Susan in Nanning

Turning and turning,
poised with my chopsticks like spears,
at awkward angles, I prepare to scissor up bits of chicken,
delicately and daintily of courses, as the table rotates,
I watch
delicious
       food
              on plates
                      pass by.

I take one bite, miss the next dish.
Our table turns and turns,
watching the plates and faces around us,
we talk and talk
I realize I am full.

Asian Chicken Marinade

2 tablespoons hoisin sauce
1½ red wine vinegar, rice vinegar, or dry sherry
1 tablespoon soy sauce
¼ teaspoon crushed red pepper
1 teaspoon grated or minced ginger
1 clove garlic, minced

Pour over diced chicken and marinate 30 minutes. Stir fry in hot oil with vegetables.

Tasting Menus

Spanish tapas or small plates, originating in Andalusia, have been popular for some time. There are various theories on their origins. Some say that the first tapas were crusts of bread used to shield drinks from debris and bugs. Others claim eating something while drinking made eating more enjoyable by moderating and extending the effects of alcohol. Still, others use the mini plates in tapas bars to tide them over between meals.

While visiting Barcelona, Madrid, and the Andalusian area, I saw some of the most beautiful art in the world. After one particularly exhausting day at the Prado, I was nearly cross-eyed and cross after trying to see everything. Was that painting by El Greco or Goya?

On the way back to our hotel, we sat outdoors with other diners and ordered tapas. When Clay asked where the restrooms were, the waiter brought him a coke. Perhaps he looked thirsty. (We are language limited though we know those basic words for toilets in Spanish.) When the tapas came, they were a feast for the eyes, at that moment as beautiful as one of Picasso's still-lifes.

Hors-d'oeuvres or finger foods, another type of small plate meaning "outside the works," often make a "main course" unnecessary. This is true partly because some of these small plates are so rich. They are also satisfying because a large variety of foods are served. If bread and fruit and vegetable trays supplement the hors-d'oeuvres, few would need to sit down to meat and potatoes after. Often small plates are nibbled while walking around or sitting by a coffee table. One evening in the Netherlands, Clay and I feasted on a vegetarian tasting menu. The small tasty bites, smaller than many appetizers, provided one of the most memorable meals I have ever eaten.

The beauty of hors-d'oeuvres, appetizers, tapas, or small plates is being able to order or serve more than one, making a meal of them. It's enjoyable to taste the variety of dishes and flavors, making it almost unnecessary to nibble from your neighbor's plate. I eat three meals daily but often nibble between them—on peanut butter, crackers, fruit, yogurt, and cereal, though for me "snackification" doesn't take the place of a dinner. That's why I was curious about the message we received when we made our reservation, while we were still in the States, for a Monday evening at a B&B, Herberg de Kop Van'T Land, in the Netherlands. The e-mail communication from the innkeeper and chef said Monday night would be a vegetarian tasting menu.

Our first night in the Netherlands in Amsterdam we had a dinner, not of small plates but larger bites at a charming restaurant called Senz. We were on our way to a concert at the Concertgebouw following the dinner. Shortly after the sumptuous dinner, our waiter shooed us out of the restaurant because he thought we were lingering too long over coffee and wouldn't be able to get to the concert on time.

We had come from driving on the Afsluitdijk, a dike thirty or so kilometers long that closes off what was the Zuiderzee from the Nordzee and which gave Friesland much of its land back. Herberg de Kop Van'T Land, the B&B, was located on Zeedijk, out in the country but not in a remote area. Sheep grazed on the grassy slopes as we wound our way to the inn. We parked behind five cars on the side of the road before walking to the door.

We settled in our room on the second floor and read our books. Our window had a good view of the river Merwede. We watched the ferry come, delivering passengers to a park on an island. Soon we walked down to the dining room where there were approximately ten tables.

The waiter told us we would be having ten small plates. The first one and the ones that followed were very small—no more than a few bites, but the flavors of each were heavenly. The first, two roasted strawberries with balsamic vinegar and crème fraîche, melted on our tongues. The plates that followed were no bigger, but we savored them, all unusual and delicious. I remember thinking we were having a light supper that night. What we were having was a long supper stretching into the totality of an evening, a meal not taken in quick bites but slow, each a burst of flavor. The meal was the evening, and we would not have had time to attend another event like the theater if we had so planned.

The last two bites were dessert, and we were surprisingly full. When the waiter asked if we wanted coffee, we told him we wanted to take a walk on the dijk. "Oh, no problem," he said. "This table is yours. You can come back here after your walk and have your coffee." We strolled looking down both flanks of the dike and saw horses and goats enclosed in fences on the farmers' land below. Then we came back and had our coffee as the sunny summer evening finally gave up its light around ten.

In the morning, we hurried to find Sliedrecht, the town from where my mother's parents came, and returned to the B&B for a typical breakfast of breads, cheeses, jams, hard-boiled eggs, yogurt, and granola. The evening nibbles had been exceptional, but sinking one's teeth into breads and crunchy cereals was right for the morning.

We ate once more on another dijk in Volendam near Edam. As we watched the sailboats, we ate our picnic of bread and cheese, more bites but each eaten faster than the last as we made our plans to go to Leiden.

Shortly after this "dinner", we returned to Michigan and Lent. I heard people talk about what they would "give up." But the day before was Fat Tuesday when some of us indulge before we deny ourselves. When I stopped at one of my favorite groceries in Lansing, Roma's Bakery Deli & Fine Foods, to purchase some tarragon and poppy seed, I found the bakery busier than usual. People waited in line for the Paczki, pronounced Poonch-key, the deep-fried pastry filled with raspberry or custard. A local paper said Roma's expected to sell 8,000 that day, each one bulging with 600 calories and 11 grams of fat. The same newspaper article said that Quality Dairy planned to sell the pastries with 11 more flavors than the traditional two.

Someone brought the delicious treats to work, and I shared one with another employee, figuring that way I'd consume only 300 calories. They reminded me of the fresh jelly doughnuts a "bread man" often delivered to our house when I was young. Paczki was made for opening the mouth wide and taking big bites.

Large portions are sometimes served in the Netherlands too. Not all meals are tasting menus. The tasting menu we had at Herberg de Kop Van'T Land is suitable for a long evening of enjoying different types of food and enjoying one another, like foreplay in unrushed love-making instead of a quickie. Perhaps it was so satisfying because it seemed like a denial of our fast pace of life—oddly indulgent of time—a commodity we feel is scarce. Small bites consumed over a long time with the emphasis on time may be the healthier way to eat.

I suspect indulging has less to do with hunger for paczki or any other fat treats and more to do with other matters. Perhaps the winter stretching into March with snow and ice is to blame. Like bears waking from the hibernation of our homes, we long to bite into something fatty, starchy, chocolaty, or sweet as honey. Or we want to shop for something that reminds us of spring when we don't have the money for new shoes or can't justify another pair. Or maybe we are lonely, and paczkis remind us of someone baking for us in our childhood. Except for Fat Tuesday, we ride waves of guilt after justifying treats one day and vowing to make up for it the next by eating rabbit food.

Maybe we feel another emptiness or deprivation we can't seem to fill regardless of how much we eat, shop, or accumulate, and Lent seems like more denial, a bitter, acidic time to deny ourselves, almost like swallowing vinegar when we are thirsty. We are relieved at Easter with its signs of spring abundance and fecundity—lambs, ham, and small bites of chocolate eggs and bunnies.

The following are some of my favorite small bites and appetizers. When served with a plate of fresh vegetables or fruits and breads, they make fine lunches and small meals.

Salmon Spread

1 14-ounce can red sockeye salmon, drained, skin and bones removed
¼ cup or more snipped oil-packed sundried tomatoes, drained
1 teaspoon anchovy paste, optional
2 cloves garlic, minced
3 teaspoons capers, drained
2 tablespoons lemon juice
2 tablespoons mayonnaise
½ teaspoon pepper

1. In a food processor, combine all ingredients.
2. Process until smooth and chill. Makes 1⅓ cups.

Easy and good with crackers and raw vegetables. Or slather it on whole grain bread with cream cheese, lettuce, and sliced cucumbers with some dill.

Herb-Marinated Goat Cheese

1-11-ounce log of soft goat cheese, cut crosswise into ⅓ inch rounds
1 clove garlic, sliced
5 chopped briny black olives
3 chopped marinated artichoke hearts, drained
Fresh thyme sprigs
Fresh rosemary sprigs
1 bay leaf
Extra virgin olive oil

1. Arrange cheese in a serving bowl. Scatter with garlic, vegetables, and herbs.
2. Add enough olive oil to cover. Refrigerate to marinate for one day. Bring to room temperature before serving with crackers. Makes 8 servings.

Adria L. Libolt

My Tapenade

1 small jar (7.5 ounces or smaller) marinated artichokes, drained
½ cup sun-dried tomatoes in oil, drained
½ cup pitted kalamata olives
2 tablespoons drained capers
1 clove chopped garlic
2 tablespoons lemon juice

Place all ingredients in a food processor or chopper and chop until fine but not pureed.
This is a great spread for baguettes, crackers, or toast. Add a piece of ham, cheese, or an egg. It packs a punch of great flavor. I've also added a teaspoon to a salad and mixed it in at the same time as I dress the greens.

Prayer:
Lord, thank you for small bites of food. Help us to savor mindfully the food you provide.

5

Finger Foods—The Right Touch

"Fingers were made before knives and forks."
—Old adage
Whoever eats my flesh and drinks my blood has eternal life...
—John 6: 53

When Mom began losing weight, my sisters and I realized she had lost interest in cooking and perhaps eating alone. The retirement housing where she had an apartment provided her meals in a dining room. Waiters and waitresses served lunch and dinner to the residents seated at tables together. Only breakfast was a buffet, and residents went through a line for their oatmeal, fruit, toast, or rolls and juice and coffee.

Residents received monthly menus so they knew what choices they would have each day. I used to ask Mom what she'd had for lunch. If she had forgotten, she would laugh and say, "Food." I would look at the menu and see what had been served. "Oh, yeah," she'd say. "We had that."

Sundays were different. The wait staff served the main meal at noon, and in the evening, residents moved through a buffet line for what was called "finger foods." Mom spoke of finger foods with some disdain as though fingers were on the menu. It's not as though she was unacquainted with the concept. At home when we were growing up, we occasionally had finger foods like chips, cookies, bars, quick breads and cake, items we picked up with our fingers from trays and cookie jars. Small plates and appetizers seem designed for picking up with the fingers. But in this case, there was a tool that came between her and finger food, namely tongs, those items that look like forceps and keep us from offending other diners. When I dined with her one Sunday evening, I followed her through the line and watched her having a devil of a time picking up deviled eggs with the tongs. I would not have done any better with those tongs. Spoons aren't much of an improvement. The eggs are slippery eels; they roll right off spoons, and plates, too. I sympathize and think I could lose my appetite fishing for food with tongs too.

When one of our nephews was young, he picked up the noodles on his plate with his fingers at a restaurant. As parents do, we said, "Joey, eat with your fork," to which he replied, "Somehow it tastes better without the fork." We use our fingers to pick up small pieces of food, like appetizers, from small plates, and sometimes even when we eat on big plates—though pasta is hardly the meal to eat without forks.

I have been to parties where buffet lines have those cute and tasty little hors-d' oeuvres begging to be picked up by the fingers and popped into the mouth, only to find someone had moved the tongs to another appetizer elsewhere. And those instruments do keep us from grabbing food every which way, but it's far easier with fingers. Yet, the thought of everyone picking up their morsels without the intervening instrument is hardly appetizing. One of my germs or one of yours could land on one of the canapés and spread to another guest. Not that bacteria or a virus couldn't spread to an appetizer via the tongs, but we keep a bit of distance from food by using them.

We have removed ourselves far from our food in ways other than using tongs. Few of us can follow the path from growing and then preparing a potato to eating it as Nigerians do. They dig the yam out of the ground, pound it, and then eat it, often using their fingers. We don't know where our food comes from or how it's produced unless we are growing it ourselves, which is rare. Even if we occasionally pick some tomatoes or peppers from a plant we've grown, or pluck some wild berries from a bush, few of us can say that we live off the land.

We eat as though we were at a party. Our buffet table offers rich specialties from all over the world, whether they are in season or not, and the food we reach for seems to be at our fingertips. We don't know the people who planted or grew the food, prepared it, or even those who serve it. We don't know the true costs of what it takes for food to reach us. We can't say we are in touch with our food, and we delude ourselves if we think having all this food so readily available makes for rich and abundant living.

Ignorance comes between us and our food. Norman Wirzba, who teaches a class on eating and the life of faith at Duke Divinity School, writes that "Today's average eater is likely the most ignorant eater in history" (Wirzba 2012, 24). He asks his students to think about the relationship between our demand for fast, cheap food and the high costs of eroded and poisoned soil, the vast quantities of fossil fuels required to produce and transport the food, abused animals and farm workers, and the poorly paid food service workers. He says, "Our cheap food comes at a very high cost." He claims that relatively few people know what it takes to provide sustainable, safe, and nutritional food. Shouldn't our ignorance make us ashamed?

Many others have written about the problems with our fast food nation (Schlosser 2001). Paul Roberts in *The End of Food* also describes the huge costs and the destructiveness of modern food production (Roberts 2008, 220-221) and about how quickly food-borne illnesses can spread with food grown far away, randomly inspected, and moved to groceries and restaurants. We are often warned about the destructiveness of the food industry and our eating practices. While such food is cheaper and easier to acquire, our food industry, with its emphasis on speed, efficiency, uniformity, and profitability, contributes to obesity, while many people in the world do not have enough to eat. Some people are not "touching" food enough or the right kinds of food. One-seventh of the population in the world, according to Roberts, is malnourished—proof that the modern food economy is failing. Bread for the World claims "862 million stomachs are growling with hunger."

Wirzba reminds us to aspire to Acts 4:34, "There was not a needy person among them."

Many problems in our food world, whether they are due to the status quo, inertia, politics, or big moneyed and powerful corporations, seem insurmountable. Even when we know more about how our food is processed and where it comes from, what can we do about it? Once we leave to others the tasks of growing, processing, and distributing food, staying knowledgeable and avoiding the problems associated with industrialized production is overwhelming for the average person.

Our alienation from the very land we depend upon keeps us from connecting to creation. If we stand apart from rather than be an integral part of a community with others human and non-human, our environment will continue to suffer. Unless we become responsible caregivers and turn from our destructive plundering of resources for our profit and our benefit alone, we cannot live. Our dependence on the land and those who farm it is total (Berry 1990).

Wirzba reminds us that the Lord's Supper, where we are touched by God in the basic bread and wine, calls us to live in creation unselfishly connected to each other and responsible for others including their hunger and appetite for new life (Wirzba 2012, 27).

I think of the bread and wine (or grape juice) at Lord's Suppers in various churches, how different each experience is, and yet how comforting the commonality between them is too. In some churches, there is only minimal contact between members of the congregation as bread and wine or grape juice are passed down rows from one person to another. When Clay and I attended an Easter service in Avignon, for the Lord's Supper everyone gathered around the walls of the cathedral, and the bread and a chalice of wine were passed around. The person who received the bread before me broke off a piece and gave it to me—fed me, you could say—and then passed the wine cup. We smiled as we took the bread and wine. Without understanding the words, we had worshipped and shared a meal with Christians across the ocean. Though the ritual was familiar, that a stranger offered me bread and wine moved me. We don't need to speak another language to understand the Lord's Supper. Feeding and being fed in this ritual gives us the example of how to share our resources in everyday life.

After being members of a large church, my husband Clay and I now often attend a small church and participate in the communion service that is a central part of the worship service. Two people bring bread and wine to the altar. The wine is in a flask and the bread, made by church members, rests on a plate. Once our vicar has received the food and drink, she begins the call and response of the "Great Thanksgiving," *"The Lord be with you."* And we respond, *"And also with you." "Lift up your hearts." "We lift them up to the Lord." "Let us give thanks to the Lord our God." "It is right to give him thanks and praise."* To and fro it goes.

After we sing the "Sanctus," she chants, half-singing, *"Therefore we proclaim the mystery of faith,"* and we all respond, *"Christ has died. Christ is risen. Christ will come again."* And then she continues with more words of the Great Thanksgiving, and we pray the Lord's Prayer. We remember Christ's suffering, we're invited to the table, and we are grateful that He touched us in this way with a meal. The disciples recognized the risen Christ by touching his wounds and again when he blessed bread and ate with them. Such is the power of the sacrament that knowing hunger, we recognize Jesus, and are invited to the meal (Luke 24: 30-31).

Sara Miles, an atheist at the time, walked into a church in San Francisco, was passed bread and wine and, "got Jesus." She says, "Jesus happened to me."[18] The sacrament changed her life. She became a part of a community that feeds the hungry. Does the Eucharist have the power to make us remember how to feed each other and see our connections? Miles took the sacrament seriously and gave of herself—her particular skills

---

[18] (Miles 2007)

and talents as a cook—so others could flourish.

Not everyone comes to feeding others in this way, walking into a church and taking Jesus in the Lord's Supper. I know people concerned about the food industry and the problems associated with it that provide food and other services to others like Miles without the Eucharist, or even a church. Many of them work in soup kitchens, food banks, and community assistance programs, distributing cans and packages of food, giving of their time, and feeding the hungry. Some like Sara Miles have the skills and talents to feed people with what satisfies hungry stomachs. For others, sacrificial giving may involve volunteering to teach or counsel someone, hiring an unemployed person, or repairing and building houses. However, we enlist our talents, the goal is the same as in Acts: that there be *"not a needy person among them."*

Meanwhile, coming to the table weekly is a tangible reminder. Offering ourselves and receiving from others blurs the lines between food for the body and food for the soul. Some would call the weekly feast a ritual, but it reminds me of who grows, prepares, and serves food, and that I'm connected to others and called to serve.

While it is silent, we walk to the table and stand side by side, bodies touching. We reflect on how we are fed. I hold out my hands. The vicar is saying, "Christ's body was broken for you," and she gives me a small piece of bread from the loaf—with her fingers—no plastic gloves, forceps, tweezers, or slippery tongs. I take it with my fingers, and while eating, the cup comes around. The touching, the weekly feast, the reflection: all these remind us of our dependence on the soil, the weather, and others for our food, and beyond that, on the One who provides all good things for us. We are hungry for food that endures. It is the right touch.

Communion Bread

3 cups whole wheat flour, preferably King Arthur brand
1¼ teaspoon baking powder
1¼ teaspoon salt
⅓ cup olive oil
⅓ cup honey
⅓ cup molasses
¾ cup boiling water

Preheat oven to 350 degrees.
1. Mix first 3 dry ingredients together.
2. Using a 2-cup measuring cup, slowly add the oil and mix. Do not wash out the cup.
3. Add the molasses and honey to the cup and fill to 1½ cups with the boiling water. Mix together.

4. Mix with the flour using a wooden spoon. Mix well. It may seem too moist at first but will soon be the right consistency.
5. Divide into 6 pieces. Place on a big plate and then flour a surface and roll each piece out to a 5-inch round.
6. Place parchment on 2 cookie sheets, place 3 loaves on each cookie sheet and brush loaves with a little olive oil.
7. Make a cross on each loaf with a very sharp knife.
8. Bake for 10 minutes brushing with more olive oil, just covering the surface of each.
9. Place in oven again for 7 minutes.
10. Cool and place each one carefully sealed in freezer bags and then in one large freezer bag until ready to use.

Focaccia

1½ teaspoons of active dry yeast
2½ cups bread flour. (I replace 1 cup with whole wheat flour.)
1 teaspoon salt
2 tablespoon vegetable oil
1 cup water
1 tablespoon cornmeal
1 tablespoon olive oil
1 teaspoon coarse kosher salt
1 teaspoon dried rosemary
1 teaspoon dried basil

1. Mix yeast, salt, vegetable oil, and slightly warm water, and then mix in the flour. (OR place these ingredients in a bread machine on the dough cycle and go to step 3.)
2. Cover the dough and let it rise in a warm place until doubled in size.
3. Remove the dough and preheat the oven to 450 degrees.
4. Flatten the dough in an 11" by 16" pizza pan or divide for two smaller pans.
5. Cover the dough with a clean towel and let rise 5 minutes.
6. Make dimples in the dough.
7. Drizzle half the olive oil over each focaccia and sprinkle with salt, basil, and rosemary. (I also add herbs *after* it comes out of the oven, like fresh oregano and thyme.)
8. Bake for about 15 minutes until crust is nicely browned.

Eat this crusty bread with your fingers.

Note: The recipe above is adapted from *The Best Bread Machine Cookbook Ever* by Madge Rosenberg (Harper Collins Publishers, 1992).

Prayer:
Lord, we are hungry for your touch. Thank you that you have blessed us in the wine and breaking of the bread and reminded us of our connection to creation. We pray that our own contact with the world reveals a taste for renewal in You.

Adria L. Libolt

FOOD ADVICE

6

Sgt. Peppers

"The way we eat is not a symbol of natural order but of a community of belief."
—Adam Gopnik [19]

When my husband Clay and I moved to Ann Arbor, Michigan in the 1970s for him to begin a Ph.D. program in Ancient Near Eastern Languages and Literature, we often went to picnics and potlucks with his colleagues. The Department was small, and everyone knew each other. The foods his friends brought seemed exotic and delicious. The table was loaded with tabbouleh, hummus, moussaka, Syrian bread, and eggplant spreads—dishes with which I was not familiar. When one of the department chairs about our age looked at the dish I'd

---

[19] (Gopnik 2011, 110)

brought, he said, "It's good to see potato salad at a picnic."

I incorporated "Near Eastern" dishes into my cooking gradually, but a small convenience store at the end of our street called Sgt. Peppers, (like the Beatles' song, Sgt. Pepper's Lonely Hearts Club Band), was a catalyst for the Near Eastern changes in our meals. Two different Palestinian men assisted the customers, and I always enjoyed talking with them. I had purchased a cookbook they were selling, and one day when I was making hummus, long before it was popular, I realized I was out of garlic, and went to the store. "How much garlic do you use in hummus?" I asked.

"A bulb," one of them said. "The more, the better."

"No, no," said the other, his voice raised. "A little is enough. You don't use a whole bulb." He placed his index finger close to his thumb, leaving a small space to demonstrate a small piece.

The argument continued, but I think the fight was about the difference in meaning between bulb and clove. I opted for a clove. I love garlic, but like many foods, one can get too much of a good thing. (I have eaten nearly a whole bulb of garlic but only when it has been drizzled with oil, wrapped in foil, and baked about an hour at 325 degrees in an oven. The skin will come off easily, and the buttery garlic paste is good when spread on some crusty French bread. Try it.)

Before the garlic discussion with the two men, I had not consumed very much real garlic. Most of my garlic experience had been "garlic" bread likely sprinkled with garlic salt or garlic powder. I didn't know what I was missing. Talking to those two men was like learning a new language. Becoming familiar with their food was a doorway into their culture.

Some advice about garlic:

Perhaps the food culture of my youth was too cautious or too bland for garlic. Garlic is best eaten in community when everyone is indulging. You can carry on a conversation without anyone reaching for a breath mint. No one notices your breath in a crowd of garlic lovers.

At the time of the Near Eastern picnics and the discussion of garlic, I was beginning to take in a wider world, meeting students from many different countries and finding the richness of diversity in people as well as tasting a variety of foods.

The hummus from the recipe below is delicious on Syrian bread or any kind of flat, crunchy bread.

Adria L. Libolt

Hummus

(Garbanzo Bean Dip)

6 cups cooked or 3 cans (15 ounces each) garbanzo beans, drained
1 cup water
Lemon juice to taste (a tablespoon or two)
Green onions, chopped
¼ teaspoon cayenne pepper
6 cloves of garlic, pressed (add a bulb if you want—at your own risk!)
1 teaspoon salt to taste but skip if you've used the canned beans
Black pepper to taste

1. Boil beans in their own juice for 5 minutes, adding water only if necessary to cover the beans.
2. Drain beans and mash, or grind them up with the garlic in a food processor, adding water when necessary.
3. Add remaining ingredients and process until smooth.
4. Place hummus on plates and garnish with paprika, parsley, and a drizzle of olive oil.
5. Serve on pita bread or as a dip for vegetables.

Suggestion: Pine nuts may be added sprinkled over the hummus.

Note: This is better than commercial hummus. If you like roasted red peppers, add some chopped peppers to the hummus or process them with the beans.

7

A Middle Eastern Lunch: An Opinion Comes with That

"After a good dinner, (or lunch?) one can forgive anybody, even one's own relations."
—Oscar Wilde

If you eat at an ethnic restaurant, you may take in more than the food. Sometimes the special comes with opinions and ideas that compete with the food, giving it an interesting aftertaste. A friend and I prefer little ethnic restaurants to the chains, grills, and cafés with their predictable Caesar salads, burgers, and fries. Small ethnic restaurants are frequently tucked away in odd places and not on prime real estate where they'd get themselves noticed. We went in search of a Middle Eastern restaurant which had received a good review in the newspaper and found this Middle Eastern place behind big buildings on the main highway. The proprietor seemed to be the owner, cook, cashier, and waiter. The place was spotless.

We mentioned the positive review in the paper, and the owner said, "This place had been good for twelve years, but just now it's being noticed?" He didn't look as busy as I would have expected with all his duties, but it was 1:15 PM, and the lunch crowd likely had already left. We shared the place with only one other party—a middle-aged couple who sat across the room. The owner/waiter answered questions while taking our orders. I read the whole menu but still couldn't decide. He told me everything was good, so I ordered the combination plate that came with three samples. He was Lebanese and answered more questions about his native country, his family, and what his two children did. Since he'd mentioned a wife, I asked him if she worked with him in the restaurant. He looked at me as though I had two heads.

He told us that long ago she had said it wasn't right for him to work alone, and she'd help. He came in every day at 4 AM, and the first week she also came in at that time. The first morning of the second week she came in at two in the afternoon. He said, "Honey, you're a good cook, but you're fired."

"You fired your wife?" we asked.

In response to the surprised look on our faces, he said, "Don't misunderstand. I love women, but you can't work with them." More surprised looks on our part. He had put his foot in his mouth but was oblivious to our reaction to his words. But he had to return to the cash register.

About that time, I noticed the couple across the room stand up to leave. The man went to pay for their meal. The woman with him walked out of her way to pass our table. With a little grin and confidential tone, she turned to us and said, "Let's jump him."

We laughed as she walked towards the door, knowing that sometimes along with the delicious, authentic hummus, tabbouleh, and kibbe, you may be served a taste of someone's culture somewhat different than your own—a combination plate with food you like and comments you'd rather leave behind like the piece of wilted lettuce I left on my plate.

Tabbouleh

1 cup fine burghul (cracked or wheat)
(I have cooked quinoa and used it in place of the burghul with no soaking necessary)
6 large tomatoes
1 bunch green onions, finely chopped
2 bunches parsley, finely chopped
2 cucumbers, diced
½ to 1 cup chopped mint leaves
½ cup crumbled feta cheese, optional
Olive oil, lemon juice, and salt to taste

1. If the recipe is made a few hours before serving, wash the burghul in a large bowl and add all the chopped vegetables, starting with the tomatoes.
2. Add dressing and mix well. This allows the burghul to absorb the natural juices of the vegetables and dressing. Otherwise, soak the burghul for 20 to 30 minutes before adding chopped vegetables and dressing.

Suggestion: Peel a lemon, dice it, and add to the tabbouleh in addition to the lemon juice.
Note: A friend suggested adding a boiled egg chopped up in a serving of tabbouleh with some added hummus. It's delicious.

Prayer:
Lord, we thank you that we can laugh with people and enjoy foods from other cultures. We pray that we will become more tolerant of people of other ethnicities and our often-unexpected differences.

8

Beef for Real and Sausage

"Laws are like sausages; it is better not to see them being made."
—Otto von Bismarck

"I do adore food. If I have any vice, it's eating. If I was told I could only eat one food for the rest of my life, I could put up with sausage and mash forever."
—Colin Baker

Because I didn't have any cassoulet while in France on my first visit, I decided to make it after we returned home. I have combined at least three recipes, and still modify how I make the dish, depending on my mood or what is in the market or my refrigerator. In fact, I vary most of the ingredients but seldom compromise on one of the items: smoky, garlicky andouille sausage. I use andouille sausage in paella and jambalaya too, and they are the better for it even when it's not called for in the recipe.

Until recently, the best andouille sausage I have tasted had been available at a meat market where I shopped. One day I did not find it in its usual place in the cooler, so I walked to where the meat personnel and butchers stood behind the counter. I had heard about the man named "Beef" who made the sausages, and I wanted to know who he was. I asked the older gentleman with a cowboy hat if he were Mr. Beef.

"It's *Doctor* Beef," he said, and then he told me he wasn't just any butcher cutting meat and tossing spices together, but he experimented on his chorizo and other sausages and tested the type and amount of spices he used and asked people who were familiar with chorizo and other sausages to taste them. He also informed me that his meat market was authentic, not an ordinary grocery that received meat from some meat "factory" where it was packaged and sold en masse.

I was chastised once more when I asked him a second question—the calorie/fat one. How many calories and how much fat do these sausages have? Of course, heh, heh, I asked not for myself, but in the event one of my guests would inquire. Could he please tell me? He didn't hesitate.

"That's ridiculous. If people are so worried about fat, they should eat less and move their chairs away from the table."

I had to agree. If you're going to have sausage, why worry about calories? Most people don't fancy rubbery low-cal turkey sausages. Get Dr. Beef's andouille sausage. Go whole hog.

The last few years I've often asked his advice about particular cuts of meat and how to cook them. I am not a big meat eater and figure I may as well get what I like when I do splurge on a chunk of meat. I noticed his response was suspiciously similar each time I asked him, always something like: it's very good baked slowly with a little brown sugar, soy sauce, and Dijon mustard. I have one in the oven right now. Right.

Although I trusted Dr. Beef's expertise, I developed a perverse habit of asking him questions to see his reaction. After all, I'm a customer. As much as he might like to remind me that my questions are silly, his withering looks are all he dares. One day I told him I'd read that farm-raised salmon were naturally gray and dyed a salmon color to make them attractive to customers. "No," he said, "they are fed carrots, and it makes them the color of wild salmon."

I've asked him why they label some meats offal; it sounds so close to "awful." I've asked him why some packages of meat have on their label, "miscellaneous." Who buys miscellaneous meat?

One afternoon I picked up a nice-looking hunk of pork and, after reading the label, walked directly to the meat counter. Dr. Beef in his white apron stood in the center, a young meat man on each side of him.

"Dr. Beef," I asked. "This label says shoulder butt. How can a piece of pork be both a shoulder and butt at the same time when they are quite far apart on the animal?"

The two young men laughed and turned to him and said, "Yeah, Dr. Beef, how can that be?"

He grinned. He may have cleared his throat, but I thought I heard him groan.

I know he waited for his opportunity, and he took it one day when I walked to the meat counter to buy fresh fish—the kind that has not been frozen and thawed.

"Dr. Beef, is the walleye good grilled?" A few other customers had gathered around the counter.

"Of course," Dr. Beef said with confidence. "Anything can be grilled. You can grill a peanut butter and jelly sandwich if you want." One customer laughed.

I wanted to ask him when he had become an expert on peanut butter and jelly sandwiches. Instead, I said, "I know. I do it all the time. I have one right now in my George Foreman Grill." I'm surprised he didn't say he had one at home in his oven, baking in some brown sugar, soy, and Dijon.

When we moved to Washington State, I greatly missed Dr. Beef. The feeling may not be mutual. I have yet to find andouille sausage as spicy and delicious as Dr. Beef's.

The following recipe has borrowed from at least three different recipes, so now I have it the way I like it.

Cassoulet

Serves 8-10

2 tablespoons olive oil
2 lbs. of smoked sausages (I use andouille)
4 large onions, thinly sliced
10 large garlic cloves
1 apple, chopped
1 tablespoon chopped fresh rosemary
1½ teaspoons dried sage
½ cup brandy
2 14-ounce cans of diced tomatoes
3 15-ounce cans of Great Northern, navy, or cannellini beans
1 10-ounce package of frozen baby lima beans or butter beans, thawed

Food: An Appetite for Life

1 red pepper, chopped (if desired)
1 cup canned chicken broth
3 tablespoons tomato paste
½ teaspoon each of thyme and sage

Topping
4 cups diced country-style bread
1 lb. tomatoes, seeded and diced
½ cup chopped fresh parsley
¼ cup olive oil

1. Preheat oven to 350 degrees. Heat 2 tablespoons oil in a heavy large oven-proof pot over medium heat. Add sausages; sauté until brown, about 25 minutes. Transfer to plate and cut into ½ inch rounds.
2. Add onions and garlic to same pot. Sauté until beginning to soften, about 8 minutes. Mix in apple, rosemary, and sage. Add brandy and simmer until almost evaporated, about 5 minutes.
3. Mix in canned tomatoes with juices, canned beans with ½ cup reserved liquid, lima beans, 1 cup broth, tomato paste, and cloves. Add sausages. Season with pepper.
4. Bring cassoulet to boil.
5. Cover pot and transfer to oven; bake 30 minutes.
(Can be made up to 2 days ahead. Uncover; cool 1 hour. Refrigerate until cold; cover and keep refrigerated.
6. Before continuing, rewarm in a covered pot in 350-degree oven for 40 minutes, adding more broth if dry.)
7. Heat ¼ cup oil in a heavy large skillet over medium heat. Add bread and sauté until golden brown, stirring often, about 25 minutes.
8. Combine fresh tomatoes and parsley in large bowl; mix in bread. Season the topping with salt and pepper. Spoon onto warm cassoulet.
9. Bake uncovered 15 minutes more.

Prayer:
Lord, thank you for Dr. Beef's advice, his andouille sausage, and for peanut butter sandwiches, plain or grilled.

9

Turkeys—Cheep and Cheaper

"He (the turkey) is besides, though a little vain and silly, a bird of courage..."
—Ben Franklin

The first year Clay and I were married, we were students going to college two thousand miles from home. Going "home" on the weekend for our moms' cooking was not an option. We were both the oldest kids in our families, so our parents had our siblings to raise; we didn't depend on them much. They liked to say about us that we were poor but happy. We could have qualified for food stamps and other available aid, but we did not think of ourselves as poor.

In the days before I knew many meatless recipes, I'd buy a pound of hamburger, divide it into thirds, and freeze two pieces before sautéing and adding the remainder to casseroles. I made penny casserole, a concoction of sliced wieners with potatoes, Campbell's soup, and other vegetables. Yes, I know, but it was in a church cookbook. We purchased large quantities of corn, peas, and beans, all cheap.

Food: An Appetite for Life

Clay worked at a factory that made shampoo and non-prescription drugs like aspirin, for pharmacies. The bonus at Thanksgiving was a turkey. Although I had never roasted a turkey, when we were given a free one at Thanksgiving, I knew I could do it. I was not about to look a gift turkey in the mouth. The bonus at Christmas was another turkey. Clay's brother Will came to college the first year Clay and I were married. He worked at the same drug factory and gave me his bonus to cook. I developed some expertise in roasting turkeys, making three of them by our first Christmas.

I was not intimidated. I lived on a farm, although I'd rather not remember all the steps turkeys take from the farm to the table. I saw chickens butchered and Mom plucking them and singeing off their feathers on the small stove we called the trash burner where we also dried walnuts in boxes behind the stove. The turkey I received was smooth with no hint of feathers, and the whole thing was in tight plastic wrapping. Still, handling raw poultry is unpleasant once the wrapper is off. What made me pause was the small parcel wrapped in paper that I found in the cavity where the turkey's neck had been. If the pouch had not been included, I could have forgotten that a turkey came with a heart, liver, and gizzard. I'm not surprised these organs are called offal in meat departments.

But then I wondered: Did these organs belong to this particular turkey? Or did the turkeys go down some assembly line, where some worker stuffed another turkey's neck and organs in the turkey's cavity where the neck had been? Did it matter? I have noticed that some turkeys seem big for their organs, but "parts is parts," as they say. I decided not to think too much about this. I plucked out the heart and liver for simmering and cut them up for the stuffing. I discarded the neck and gizzard. We weren't that poor.

Preparing this bird for the oven gave me an opportunity to see it up close and personal. Long before I was aware of how turkeys we purchased in stores were not only plucked but plumped up by being buttered and injected with juices, what struck me is how the modern turkey has been engineered. With their insignificant heads and necks, and ample bird bodies of meat, they look as though they were designed to feed us. Ben Franklin's "silly" is a more apt description of the modern turkey than "courage." George Lang claims, "often admiring a chef and getting to know him is like loving goose liver and then meeting the goose." Perhaps it's best not to know the turkey either. They only look beautiful without their heads, when they're browned and stuffed and we are hungry. That's why a friend's story seems so amusing.

Her mother-in-law, concerned that a Thanksgiving turkey was not fully cooked, decided to speed things up a bit, so she placed the hapless bird in the pressure cooker only to have the meat cooked, certainly done, but resting on the bottom of the pot with not a sliver left on the carcass for soup. Most of us have turkey stories revealing that turkeys don't have the market on foolishness. We are what we eat, and while we eat the engineered plumped up birds of our food industry, the holidays and their potential for stress may make us as foolish as turkeys.

    A few years later, I was working at the Maxey Boys Training School. One of the teachers was known for looking for a bargain. One day close to Thanksgiving, another teacher gave him directions to a farm that sold turkeys cheap. He took the map and made his way to the farm. He had traveled a few miles and made several turns, each time seeing the sign pointing the way to the turkeys. He bumped over the ruts on the last narrow dirt road. Finally, he reached a dead end. A large sign said, "Maxey Turkeys, Sold Cheap."

    Poultry is not cheap for everyone. Although organic, pasture-fed, cage-free poultry is best for the animal and us, it is twice as expensive. Yet turkeys that come off assembly lines from our food industry poultry farms also come with expenses. Poultry plant workers' injuries are one such cost. Gabriel Thompson worked in a poultry plant and wrote about the pressure workers are under to process ninety-one birds a minute, a rate established by the US Department of Agriculture, allegedly based on food safety concerns, and estimated to save $90 million in taxpayer money over three years by reducing both the number of online inspectors and dangers to the public. However, according to Thompson, the USDA did not account for worker safety, and many people on the line developed hand problems (carpal tunnel or tendinitis) from the hard and fast work. Nor did such speed make the birds safer to eat. The USDA then allowed some plants to run lines of 175 birds a minute.

    The television channel ABC interviewed one USDA inspector trying to keep up with the speed of processing 175 birds per minute. "You just kind of watch them fly by... We're not inspecting anymore; we're kind of monitoring. We joke. We pat them on the butt and let them keep on going." Thompson asks at the end of the article, "We consider a food product safe if it's something we can feed our children. But what if producing the food does so much damage to the hands of workers that they are unable to hold their own?"[20]

    Cheaper poultry is eaten without regard to raising our animals humanely and at the expense of those who grow, harvest, and process our food. Faster is not safer for our food workers. Before we can rely on the food industry, we need to know that our workers are not paying with their limbs for our cheaper food. The National Chicken Council has refuted that the increase in processing the number of birds has jeopardized safety and claims safety for workers has increased (USDA Poultry Inspection Proposal: Separating Myth vs. Fact 2013).

---

[20] (Thompson 2012, 23-26)

About the stuffing, or dressing as it is often called: I always stuffed the raw turkey before placing it in the oven. The bird's juices bake and soak into the dressing giving it a wonderful flavor. Some cry foul because of the potential for bacteria when a raw bird is stuffed. In the last few years, I've tried brining or heating up the bird prior to stuffing it, but I may not be eliminating the risks. Putting stuffing inside of the bird, for at least some of the time it roasts, is delicious.

Choose a cage-free turkey that enjoyed life without hormones or antibiotics. While they are not cheap, turkey is not the most expensive meat. They were especially savory at one time early in our marriage when we were poor, hungry for the Thanksgivings of our parents' tables, and they seemed free but were, in fact, a part of workers' wages.

The following recipe is an old, inexpensive, and traditional dressing for turkeys. I sometimes add more apples, and less bread than the recipe calls for with equally delicious results. Enjoy.

Adria L. Libolt

Rum Raisin and Apple Stuffing for a 10-14 lb. Turkey

½ cup raisins
⅓ cup rum mixed with ⅓ cup hot water—I use almost all rum
1 loaf whole grain whole wheat, pumpernickel, or bran bread, or a combination of them (stale, if possible)
1½ cup of low-sodium chicken broth
Fresh pepper
1 teaspoon thyme
1½ teaspoon sage
½ teaspoon savory
¼ cup chopped parsley
3 medium apples, unpeeled and chopped
2 large onions, chopped (about 2 cups)
4 stalks celery, diced (about 1½ cups)
3 tablespoons margarine, melted
3 egg whites, lightly beaten

1. Place raisins in a small bowl and cover with rum and water. Marinate one hour to allow raisins to absorb the liquid.
2. If bread needs to be dried, spread slices on a rack for several hours or place in a 300-degree oven until dried, about 15 minutes. Cut bread into cubes or break into crumb size with spoon or food processor.
3. Chill chicken broth overnight in the refrigerator or one hour in the freezer to make it easier to skim off the fat. Set aside.
4. Combine bread crumbs with pepper, thyme, sage, savory, and parsley. Mix well. Add broth and beaten egg whites, apples, onions, celery, and margine. Mix again. Place dressing in a buttered casserole or spoon the stuffing into the cleaned turkey. Don't pack too tightly. Allow some space for expansion upon heating.
5. After cooking, remove stuffing to a separate bowl before carving the turkey and keep warm in a 200-degree oven until ready to serve. Makes enough for a 10-14 lb. turkey.

Prayer:
We thank you for growers, poultry workers, inspectors, and distributors. We pray for humane ways to raise poultry and safety for poultry workers and that all those parts come together in blessing rather than sacrifice. We thank you on Thanksgiving Day and always.

10

Bûche de Noël

"We don't need it, but we have it."
—Bill Yosses, White House chef, about dessert

Who am I to give advice in public about food or demonstrate how to follow a recipe? I who experiment, have flops, and lick out the frosting bowl. Yet there I stood in the church kitchen with Christmas bulbs and glitter strung out in the church for the "Mom-to-Mom" program's Christmas party. The women were celebrating with a luncheon and three Christmas workshops. Sarah, the head of the planning committee, asked me to take the Christmas baking station and demonstrate making a yummy Christmas dessert.

Sugar plums danced in my head as I thought of desserts I made during the holidays. I thought about my family's recipe for mock plum pudding. I suggested an angel food cake shaped like an angel, or a trifle minus the brandy since the dessert was to be made in church. For the same reason, rum cake was not an option here either. But Sarah had a specific dessert in mind—Bûche de Noël. I had made a pumpkin cake roll. The method was similar—a bit complicated. Already I felt the double stress of making something I'd not made before and making it for acquaintances rather than family.

Here's what you must do: Bake a cake in a jelly roll pan, so it is an even thin layer. Have ready a cookie sheet and small dish towel sprinkled with confectioner's sugar. When the cake comes out of the oven, gently place the cake on the towel (very tricky) and roll it up in the towel. Let it cool. Later unroll the cake and spread a filling on it. Fillings are usually some lush custard or mousse-like pudding. Once the filling is spread on the cake, roll it up again (trickier still). The cake is fragile.

The whole roll will look more like a log once the chocolate frosting is applied. When the log is frosted, run the tines of a fork over the frosting, length-wise, to give it the appearance of a log.

I knew many things could go wrong from the point of flipping the cake onto the towel to unraveling the roll. I decided to make two completed logs ahead of time, so if the demo flopped, those who came to my station could see how a "bûche" should look. One of the ones I baked looked more muscular. I must not have rolled it as tight as the other, or did I roll it the wrong way? (Some recipes called for rolling up the short end and others the long.) I secretly labeled it my *butch* de noël. I made white chocolate leaves for one of the bûches and added cinnamon candies for the berries. (So cute.) I spent half a day in the kitchen making the two cakes. And made the cake, filling, and frosting for the demonstration cake so all three would be ready for assembly when I arrived at the church. I also made some marzipan mushrooms (very cute) to scatter around the log. The basement refrigerator was full of two completed bûches and one in an unassembled state.

On the big day, I was very nervous. I gathered my apron, another cookie sheet, and my two completed bûches, carefully placed them in the car, and drove to church. I was early. I made several trips from my car to my station, arranging everything on the kitchen counter. I would be in the kitchen space where a sliding door opens up to the audience. Oh, no! I realized I had forgotten the demo bûche! I had just enough time to make it home and back if I hit the lights right.

At home, I gathered up the filling, frosting, and cake. I tried not to fly around corners, remembering the time I spilled the baked beans when I took a corner too fast on the way to a potluck, and the crockpot tipped on its side, spilling beans on the floor mat in my car.

I made it back with the cake all in one piece. I carried the filling and the frosting into the kitchen and for the second time set my materials on the counter, in the space of the sliding door. I was shaking. Many eager faces waited for the magic of Bûche de Noël. When I was about to unroll the cake, I realized I had inadvertently brought my worn out and ugly looking cookie sheet. With a very red face, I apologized. The women laughed and said they all had one like that at home. The cake came together beautifully, and some of the women took pictures before we rewarded ourselves with samples. I was giddy with relief.

Perhaps eating these cakes could contribute to a heart attack. In my case, my heart fluttered in anxiety for trying to create something only practice or a chef could get right. Adam Gopnik claims "we amateur cooks, though sometimes lucky, never seem to make the best meals for guests."[21] But then Bûche de Noël is not a meal. Who needs desserts? At Christmas, we may eat cookies and candies we deny ourselves the rest of the year. We are celebrating. Life may be shorter when we eat rich desserts, but it's certainly sweeter.

Recipe for Bûche de Noël

Cake
¾ cup all-purpose flour
¼ cup cocoa
1 teaspoon baking powder
¼ teaspoon salt
3 eggs
1 cup sugar
⅓ cup water
1 teaspoon vanilla

1. Heat oven to 375 degrees.
2. Line a 16 by 11 inch (or so) jelly roll pan with waxed paper or baking parchment. Grease and flour the bottom.
3. Mix flour, cocoa, baking powder, and salt. Set aside.
4. Beat eggs in small mixer bowl on high speed until very thick and lemon colored, 3-5 minutes.
5. Pour eggs into a large mixer bowl, and gradually beat in granulated sugar.
6. Beat in water and vanilla on low speed.
7. Gradually add flour mixture, beating until batter is just smooth.
8. Pour into pan, spreading batter to corners. Bake until wooden pick inserted in center comes out clean, 12-15 minutes.

---

[21] (Gopnik 2011, 143)

9. Loosen cake from edges of pan; invert on towel generously sprinkled with powdered sugar. 10. Carefully remove paper; trim crusty edges from cake if necessary.
11. While hot, roll cake and towel from narrow end.
12. Cool on a wire rack for 30-60 minutes.

Cake recipe by Barb Schaller and Betty Crocker accessed November 24, 2007, at http://www.recipezaar.com/5440

Filling
8 ounces cream cheese
8 squares of white chocolate
2 tablespoons sugar
¼ cup cream

1. Whip cream cheese until fluffy.
2. Melt the chocolate in a double boiler or the microwave.
3. Mix in the sugar and cream, and then add to the cream cheese.
4. When the cake is cool, spread the filling on it. (After step 11 above.)

Chocolate frosting
1 lb. confectioner's sugar
½ cup cocoa powder (unsweetened)
¼ teaspoon salt
¼ lb butter
6 tablespoons milk
1 teaspoon vanilla

Combine in a double boiler. Stir until smooth; remove from heat. Cool, stirring frequently. Makes a spreadable but firm icing. Frost the log, then run the tines of a fork gently over the cake to give it the appearance of a log. If desired, add decorations like marzipan mushrooms or white chocolate leaves and cinnamon candies for berries.

Prayer:
Thank you for being with us when we are nervous about making a public appearance. Thanks for church communities that understand. Thanks for the fun of cooking and baking and the joy of sharing something sweet with others.

11

Ollie Bollen

Ollie Bollen on New Year's Day, 2011

Flour, soda, egg, and chopped apple stirred and mixed
shaped into balls the size of ripe limes
dropped in a pan of sizzling oil
fried to light brown and rising to the top.
Scoop up the soft pillows, roll them in

cinnamon sugar or powdered plain,
slightly sweet, still warm, something like
coffee cake, bread, doughnut holes or fritters
not mattering, only that simple ingredients come together
and then apart in rich bites in our mouths.

On this crisp January day, our lips are laced with powdered sugar
while icicles of brittle brightness
drip at the kitchen window and
sprinkles of snow lazily fall,
luscious flakes melting, vanishing.

Lynden, Washington, my hometown with a population of just over 12,000, began with an influx of largely Dutch immigrants, and the town has capitalized on that ethnic culture. A large windmill that functions as a hotel is prominent on Front Street and can be seen several miles south in the Nooksack River bottom area of rich dairy farmland. Despite the downturn in the economy, the Dutch Mothers' restaurant serves breakfast, lunch, and dinner, and Dutch waitresses sometimes with brogues serve the restaurant's specialties including Pannekoeken (Dutch pancakes) and Erwtensoep (pea soup).

Clay and I were visiting family, especially our aging moms whom we had taken out for a New Year's Eve dinner. We drove by my favorite of the Christmas light displays along Lynden's streets, this one by the library. Several large metal skaters in a row "light up" individually very quickly giving the illusion of skaters racing across the ice. Their perpetual dance never seems to tire or age them though I suppress a yawn.

Clay's mom "Jo," who still recited poetry in her nineties, lives in a retirement apartment called Meadow Greens. My mom Ann, 85, is moving into the same apartment complex. She is glum about it. She has always been a good cook but has lost weight recently. She squints at her chicken soufflé recipe as though it is written in chicken scratches instead of a language. We find uneaten TV dinners in her freezer where frozen meat occupied space in the past. Cans of tuna replaced flour and sugar and other staples, but they are not opened either. She sets my sister's table with two knives at one place setting and two forks at another. My nephew says that when he visited Grandma, she removed a pan from the oven with a towel, and it caught on fire.

Tomorrow, on New Year's Day, we will be visiting my aunt and her family. My Uncle Mick had called. "You don't want to miss your eighty-eight-year old Aunt Priscilla making Ollie Bollen." We usually celebrate New Year's the American way, watching football. Ollie Bollen, something of a cross between doughnut holes and fritters, is an old Dutch New Year's tradition. Once they come out of the fryer, the warm balls are rolled in powdered sugar or a mixture of sugar and cinnamon. Delicious, and Mom thinks so too, but she still looks sad about moving. Mom didn't make them on New Year's Day, and now I don't think she could if she wanted to. That morning, she had forgotten her purse, and hung the same 2010 calendar because, as she said, it had the same days, and she still liked the pictures. My second Ollie Bollen makes a little lump in my throat.

Initially, Clay wasn't too excited about the visit to my aunt's either. He was more interested in foot bollen than Ollie Bollen. When I am in Lynden, I want to make family connections and make people happy, too. But Clay was a good sport; by the time we left, Aunt Priscilla's Ollie Bollen had brightened our days as though we had been given a chunk of summer sun.

When we left Aunt Priscilla's, I looked back in my Lynden recipe books, collections from schools or churches that made good shower and wedding gifts, and were given to me as a new wife, along with the instructions for some of the meals that were familiar to me. Some of the yellowed pages were frayed and loose, but two of the books had as many as five Ollie Bollen recipes, some made with quick dough, and some with yeast. I found one I had made several years ago with my typical note, "Good."

Many of the recipes had endnotes of little mottos or aphorisms sprinkled at the bottom of the pages as though the food without the words of advice could not provide all the nourishment we need. So, on a page with a recipe calling for a stiff batter, a line at the bottom read, "The yoke of God will never fit a stiff neck." A recipe calling for eggs might say, "You may have a heart of gold, but so does a hard-boiled egg." Other truths didn't have much to do with the recipe. "Children need a great deal of love, especially when they don't deserve it." "The better you know yourself, the less fault you see in others." "If you don't scale the mountain, you can't see the view," and my favorite, "Virtues are learned at mother's knee, vices at other joints."

Some of the advice reminded me of Mom. "You cannot live the maximum life with a minimum of faith." "A soft answer turneth away wrath" is characteristic of how Mom lives. Some of the plain truths we learned from Mom were meatier and homelier than clever aphorisms, like the laws of the Ten Commandments—honor your parents, tell the truth, and love your neighbor as yourself—not little snacks but lessons as rich as mashed potatoes or Ollie Bollen.

I wonder when I began giving her advice. "Are you eating enough?" "Did you have enough fruit and vegetables?" "Don't forget your purse." "You might want to wear a coat." Sometimes Mom calls me by my sister's name or forgets the name of a friend, but she never seems to forget to say, "You are so precious to me," as sweet as what an uncle used to say to her: "Annika, Annika, siroop in a cannika" (syrup in a can).

I've been thinking about advice that comes with food. Perhaps food does stick to our ribs better with a little advice—just as long as it doesn't add too many calories.

I was walking through our church's gym on a Wednesday evening when it is transformed into buffet lines and tables for our weekly community dinner. The dinner gives a break to tired cooks, and once people are eating at the church, it's easier to stay for choir and some of the classes offered after the meal. I had picked up my entrée of chicken lasagna and moved along to the table where several volunteers serving the food ladled out vegetables and other side dishes. I told Greg I'd like to try a little macaroni and cheese. "What?" He asked. "You already have lasagna. It will go right to your butt."

"Just a little scoop, a mere taste," I said. And then I looked at him and said, "What is this? Do we get advice and a helping of guilt with our food?"

I laughed. My butt, indeed. Then again, he is a doctor—a knee doctor—and probably knows a thing or two…

Ollie Bollen

4 cups of flour
4 heaping teaspoons baking powder
1 teaspoon salt
1 cup sugar
1⅓ cup milk
4 eggs (beaten)
1½ cup raisins which have been boiled in a little water and cooled
½ cup apple (chopped) optional

1. Sift dry ingredients together.
2. Add milk and eggs and mix all together.
3. Add raisins and apples.
4. Let rise a few hours. Fry in oil at 330-340 degrees until browned.

Prayer:
Lord, thanks for the sweetness of Ollie Bollen, which unites our family in a New Year's tradition.

FOOD ACCIDENTS—THE GOOD, THE BAD, AND THE EDIBLE

12

Mixing, Matching, and Accidents

"Women are like tea bags. They don't know how strong they are until they get into hot water."
—Eleanor Roosevelt

In current fashion, almost anything goes. Green blouses with blue pants are fine—at least for some. Except for my husband, Clay, who makes certain his ties have a little of the color of the jacket he's wearing, most people no longer shy away from wearing a red scarf or tie with a pink blazer or blouse. We're not as worried about being coordinated as we once were, but some limits prevail. No bold striped pants with polka dot shirts, for example.

We also have some rules about what foods are served together. Dieticians and food experts speak of "balanced" meals with a protein like meat or beans, a starch like pasta, rice, or potatoes, and a vegetable like lettuce, broccoli, or carrots. In rich countries like ours, where variety is available, color is part of the balance. We are advised to serve something green, red, or another bright color if white rice is on the plate, and to refrain from serving white potatoes, white fish, and cauliflower all on the same plate.

I worked in several prisons during my career, and part of my job entailed checking and inspecting kitchens and dining rooms where the meals were served. Dieticians who planned the meals faced a challenge when considering different dietary needs as well as balance. As I mentioned before, the diners who didn't eat meat received extra peanut butter. While peanut butter is protein, I wondered whether it washed down okay with the peas and potatoes already on the menu. One day I noticed French fries on the menu with pizza. The rationale was likely that one was a starch and one a bread. I don't know. Perhaps a comfort meal combined favorite foods. A balance of color prevailed too in the goldenness of the fries and the red tomato sauce on the pizza.

The work of food publishers who must keep coming up with creative combinations to appeal to their readers is not an enviable one. I've noticed after receiving a favorite magazine for five years that the recipes are starting to look suspiciously familiar. However, my latest issue has tomatoes and corn served in pies and custards along with dessert ingredients—a new one to me. A special page features figs served in salads and vegetable dishes.

Some of the best foods were mixed and matched by accident. In 1937 when Ruth Wakefield of Whitman, Massachusetts was missing baker's chocolate for her Butter Drop Do cookies, she used a semi-sweet chocolate bar instead, a gift from Andrew Nestlé, and chocolate chip cookies were born. When Ruth's recipe became popular, Nestlé printed the Toll House Cookie recipe on its packages, and Ruth was given a lifetime of Nestlé chocolate. Chocolate chip cookies and ice cream cones were "accidentally" invented at the St. Louis world's fair in 1904 when the vendor serving ice cream ran out of plates and had the idea to use thin waffles from another vendor, creating one of the best treats invented. Others include potato chips, cornflakes, popsicles, and raisins.

Not long ago, my husband and I sat down to dinner at Mom's with my sister Ruth, who had given her some assistance with the meal. Mom was a great cook, but for the last few years, she had been saying in different ways that she was not up to it anymore. Everything looked good with a salad and one of my favorite chicken casseroles. My sister was spooning out her portion when she looked puzzled. All of us watched in amazement as she pulled a used tea bag from the chicken and vegetables. Mom, sitting by my sister, gently tried to pluck it away from my sister and under her plate, but we were all laughing by this time, including Mom, and speculating about how the tea bag had made its way into the casserole. Did the bag slip off her cup into one of the ingredients going into the soufflé or fall from a cupboard unnoticed into the baking dish? Chicken Soufflé with Tea Bag will not make it into any cookbooks. Most accidents do not.

I told my sister she had been outdone by Mom. A few years ago, Ruth's mixer threw off a part as she made a cheesecake for a church function. Fortunately, the lady who got a metal screw with her piece of Ruth's cheesecake had a sense of humor.

A lady in my church who was making a salad for a potluck had taken the Jell-O out of the refrigerator to assemble her salad and set it on the counter. A little later she caught her cat tiptoeing through it. A foodie might describe it as "Jell-O à la cat paw print." She scooped out the paw prints in the Jell-O, and a nice thick layer of whipped cream took care of the indentations. No one was the wiser. For most of us, dropping an onion or potato on the floor and quickly recovering it is part of the game. We are just grateful that our recipes turn out as well as they do. "Who's to Know?" as Julia Child would say.

Moowiches
Serves 6

12 chocolate chip cookies, preferably homemade
Your favorite flavors of ice cream

1. Scoop or spread softened ice cream at least an inch thick all over on a cookie
2. Place another cookie on top and repeat with remaining cookies.
3. Freeze at least a couple of hours.

These are good after a barbeque. Add some chocolate
 or butterscotch sauce if you are serving these on a plate.

Chocolate Chip Pie

1. Preheat the oven to 375 degrees.
2. Sprinkle a little sugar in the bottom of an oiled 10 or 11-inch tart pan.
3. Spread out one batch of chocolate chip cookie dough, purchased or homemade,
and press up the sides of the tart pan.
4. Depending on how thin the dough is, bake it 15-20 minutes until baked like a cookie.
5. When the crust is cool, fill it with softened ice cream.

I've used vanilla, butter pecan, mint, or cherry, or use layers of different flavors. Freeze until firm. When serving, if you wish, top it with a sauce or topping. Yum.

Mom's Chicken Soufflé Casserole

1. Butter a 9 by 13-inch pan and spread with stuffing mix, or your own dried bread cubes, about 6 cups.
2. Pour over the bread or stuffing ¼ cup of chicken broth mixed with a cube of melted butter.
3. Cook 1 lb. of chicken breasts, skinless and boneless (about 4 cups of chicken)
4. Mix the chicken with some onions, ½ cup of celery, ½ cup of mayonnaise, and ½ teaspoon of salt.
5. Spread over the first layer.
6. For the third layer, beat 2 eggs and add half of the milk. Let stand for an hour.

Optional: Add a can of cream of chicken soup mixed with one cup of shredded cheese. Bake 325 degrees for 40 minutes.

Note: Very good with or without tea. Dispose of the tea bag after brewing the tea.

Prayer:
Lord, thank you for surprises with food, and for unexpected new and unlikely combinations in our foods and lives.

13

A Near Ruin by Ruam

"Indigestion is charged by God with enforcing morality on the stomach."
—Victor Hugo, French writer (1802-1885)

"Cooking connects every hearth fire to the sun and smokes out whatever gods there be—along with the ghosts of all our kitchens past, and all the people who have fed us with love and hate and fear and comfort, and whom we, in turn, have fed. A kitchen condenses the universe."[22]
—Betty Fussell

Seven of us laughed and talked about one couple's experiences while they'd lived in Nigeria for a year. They told us about the small goat named Bleat that at the end of their visit became a farewell feast for their

---
[22] (Fussell 1999)

community. "You ate Bleat?" we asked in disbelief.

In the kitchen, we were making a feast of our own: a dish called Ruam with a lot of the ingredients that people call a heart attack on a plate. It has pork, not necessarily the lean kind, peanut butter, and is fried in lots of hot palm oil heated over an open fire until it smokes (a burner turned to high on the stove would have to suffice). Other healthier ingredients include onions, spinach, and tomato paste. The whole meal is usually served with a particular Nigerian yam that is eaten by cupping it around the Ruam. Our friends told us that, except for instant potatoes made thick and stiff, there is nothing comparable in the States. We were going to use the instant potato mixture to scoop up the Ruam.

We were using a burner on the stove in the high position hoping for no catastrophe. We added the ingredients and while, enjoying our drinks, the Ruam heated up. I opened the only small window in the kitchen as the Ruam began smoking. Our guests promised this was as it should be.

My husband Clay, at the time, smoked a pipe, not gently in the relaxed way you see men in tweed jackets with patches on their elbows smoke, but with a vengeance, puffs taken in fast succession. He began coughing more and more. Smoke continued to fill the kitchen in spite of the stove fan and the wide-open window. His cough worsened, and he retreated to our bedroom and bathroom to recover. By this time, I was worried about him suffering serious smoke inhalation from the Ruam complicated by pipe smoking. I followed him, but he told me to go back down and join our guests, and that he thought he would be okay. I slopped up my Ruam with the instant potatoes along with our guests. It was delicious.

I went upstairs. Clay looked peaked but said he was ready to come down for the dessert that he had promised to make. When he got to the dining room, everyone cheered. "Okay," said one of our guests, "You didn't come down for our dinner, but we'll stay for your dessert."

"And what is it?" asked another. It was to be another fiery dish. Soon butter sizzled in the pan for Bananas Foster, his famous flaming dessert. The only things not burned that evening were calories. He squeezed the lemon in and added the bananas, followed by the liqueurs. He tipped the pan carefully, and the blue flames leaped into the pan licking up the Grand Marnier, dark rum, and brandy. When the flames went out, we slurped up the soft ice cream with the bananas with not so much as a sputter, glad for this finale and relieved that it was a flambé and that where there is fire, there is not necessarily smoke.

Ruam

1. Heat ½ jar red palm oil in large pan until it smokes.
2. Chop ½ lb. pork, then fry until it's cooked. Remove meat and turn heat down under the oil.
3. Fry an onion and several hot green peppers chopped, split lengthwise.
4. Remove when the onion is soft.
5. Add 1 large bunch chopped fresh spinach, fry a short time.
6. Add some water and 1 cup of tomato paste
7. Add 2 teaspoons soy sauce (unless doubling the recipe). Bring to boil.
8. Add 2 tablespoons peanut butter.
9. Return meat to pot and simmer. Salt to taste.

Note: I prefer making a stiff bunch of natural mashed potatoes and eating the Ruam on the potatoes rather than trying to use a stiff mixture of instant potatoes, but if that is what you have, go ahead.

Two Martinis and a Hamburger

My friend Phil tells of a near food "ruin" he had while he managed a country club. A sales manager called to ask whether the club still served the two martinis and a hamburger special for lunch. Phil assured him they did, and that he'd reserve two seats at the bar for the sales manager and his guest. Phil told the cook to fry the hamburgers exactly as ordered because the sales manager was a good customer but quite picky.

Thirty minutes later the waiter ran to his office. "There's a problem," he said and waved for Phil to follow him. Two unhappy customers sat at the bar. At first Phil thought there had been pieces of glass in the meat because the guest had fire in his eyes and his lips were a bright unnatural red as though he were bleeding. When he stuck out his tongue, he dripped red on his white shirt.

"What happened to you?" Phil asked him.

The salesman raising his voice said, "He ordered his burger rare, and the cook must have overcooked it and doctored it up with food coloring to make it appear rare. I want his ass, or I'm going to have yours and the entire board of directors for this."

Phil apologized and saw the bottle of red food coloring on the counter in front of the broiler and the cook acting as if nothing out of the ordinary had happened. When Phil asked him what he had done to the man's hamburger, the cook's explanation came out slurred.

"He wanted it rare, so I helped it along a little to make it look like he wanted it. That's all."

When Phil accused him of being drunk, the cook denied it but said that he thought two martinis and a hamburger special sounded good and he'd tried one himself.

Phil fired him, went back to the bar, and apologized once more to the customers.

The cook eventually got his job back on the grounds that when Phil had originally hired him, he had not given him written notice that he could not get drunk on the job.

Prayer:
Keep us humble and gentle with the food we prepare and those who consume it.

14

Shaping a Signature Dish: More on Hamburger

Recipes are made to evolve, and we are made to improvise. (My kitchen motto.)

Most of the family, except for the happy couple who left on their honeymoon, gathered around our table on the patio for a light supper. I wasn't very hungry, because the wedding had been followed by a generous dinner reception. I was sleepy and hadn't prepared for a meal for my sister's family, including nieces, who had been bridesmaids, and their boyfriends.

By this time, the boutonnières that had been pinned on tuxedos for half a day were drooping, and the bridesmaids had substituted their high heels for flip-flops. The frenetic chatter of the day had settled into quiet kidding. My husband, Clay, turned on the grill, and I opened a big package of hamburger and shaped it into no-frills patties. We pulled one salad from the refrigerator and made another while the hamburgers sizzled on the grill. After devouring all that, we had ice cream for dessert, and most of the family left for their motel and flights home the next day.

Later, I learned that one of my nieces had laughed about the small hamburgers she said were about the size of my hand. Are they making bread buns bigger these days? I had not intended to stretch the meat and leave the guests with a ridge of bread to sop up the catsup. I once had one of those plastic hamburger molds that make uniform flat hamburgers, but it likely was packed away along with the omelet maker in a box when we moved years ago, and I'd decided that we could eat perfectly good hamburgers and omelets without devices designed for one purpose only. I use my George Foreman grill more for Panini and sandwiches than hamburgers. Anything that's going to have a spot in my cupboard has to have more than one culinary function.

I was a bit defensive. My palm-shaped hamburgers were rough around the edges and a little fatter in the middle than those made in a hamburger maker. Though not professional, they were perfectly fine hamburgers. And yes, like all signature meals, they reflected the hand of the cook.

I am reminded of the time I asked one of my colleagues for a recipe. I looked it over, and said, "I think I'll use raspberries instead of the blueberries, and could one use yogurt instead of the sour cream? Oh, and I may use vanilla wafers instead of the graham cracker crumbs."

She looked amused and said, "I usually follow the recipe the first time before making substitutions."

Not me. I want to make it mine right off the bat. Sometimes the authors of recipes wouldn't recognize "their" dish by the time I set it on the table. My advice is to tinker and taste. Individualize. You can always improve it. Add the hottest new spice. Think outside the catsup bottle and hamburger shaper. Chipotle hamburgers are delicious, and they taste good regardless of their shapes. Recipes are made to evolve, and we are made to improvise.

Recipes that flop can be delicious. Food that doesn't have the same shape it had on the magazine picture say it's uniquely mine or yours!

Several years ago, twenty-five new people from church came over for a get-acquainted coffee. I had the perfect cake recipe that served twenty-five, and it had many of my favorite things—white chocolate, raspberry and blackberry filling, and buttercream frosting—baked and decorated in the shape of a woman's hat. I'd had the recipe for years. I followed the recipe except I used my 10-inch spring-form pan instead of an 11-inch cake pan. Baking a cake is not a time to improvise in any serious way, but the bottom layer turned out fine. The top layer was from an 8-inch spring-form pan. The cake had my signature.

On the picture in the magazine, the cake was a perfect hat, the bottom layer larger than the top with a ribbon wrapped around the bottom of the top layer, with blackberries and raspberries on the top. The frosting was piped on in little beads all the same size in perfect shapes. I'm not a professional cake decorator; I don't do piping or beads. A generous amount of the frosting ran all over the cake obscuring the two cake layers, but I was not about to waste a spoon of it. Even with all the frosting, it looked like a hat, albeit a very floppy hat. But it was not a flop: like my hamburgers, it was delicious, and not a piece was left.

Perhaps I'll buy a hamburger mold. The hamburgers will be too flat to include surprises, but use of the mold won't be limited to hamburgers. It'll do nicely for perfectly uniform cookies. Once the cookies are made, ice cream can be shaped in the hamburger shaper to match the size of the cookies for ice cream sandwiches. Kids can use them too. The mud pies my sister and I used to make, decorated with daisies and violets, were about the size of the mold. Just saying.

Surprise Hamburgers

1 lb. of hamburger, ground beef, or turkey or a mixture of these
Sliced red roasted peppers from a jar
Sun-dried tomato slices packed in oil from a jar
Pimento stuffed olives, optional
Mozzarella cheese in thin slices

1. Shape hamburgers into patties. Try not to use a hamburger shaper.
2. In the middle of each hamburger, slip a roasted pepper slice or sundried tomato and a slice of cheese, covering it on all sides with the meat.
3. Salt and pepper them.
4. Grill them to your liking or fry them.

Note: They will not make your mouth turn red unless a piece of pepper or tomato sticks to your teeth.

I wonder how we are shaped by what and how we eat. How do we shape our world by what foods we eat?

Prayer:
Lord, you shape us as we continue to grow and change. Thank you for making each of us unique, each with special gifts, yet all made in your image.

15

The Luck of the Pot

*"Sharing food with another human being is an intimate act
that should not be indulged in lightly."*
....—MFK Fisher

Nancy Barnwell, wife of the British pastor, Reverend Ainsley Barnwell, told of the time he was preaching a sermon and had been reminded to announce the potluck which would take place the following week. He ended his sermon and then said, "And oh, don't forget to bring something for the lucky pot next week."

I had assumed that the word "potluck," referring to the prepared food brought by people to share with others who have likewise brought food, came from the word, "potlatch," "a ceremonial feast among certain Native American peoples of the northwest Pacific coast, as in celebration of a marriage or accession, at which the host distributes gifts according to each guest's rank or status." This definition seemed somewhat in keeping with the concept of today's potluck especially since the potluck is often a gathering of people, involves a feast and sharing, and seems to have some roots in the Pacific Northwest. However, the origins of the word "potluck" actually derive from sixteenth-century England usage and mean "food provided for an unexpected or uninvited guest, 'the luck of the pot,'" a definition that reminds me of Pastor Ainsley's lucky pot. An Irish variant of potluck came from cooks who used one pot for cooking whatever food was available that day. (Potlatch n.d.)

Many potlucks are held in dining rooms of churches, and the recipes for the homey dishes are often included in church cookbooks. Restaurant fare and the potluck share the adventure of trying something new that someone other than you cooked or baked. The sharing of each other's food goes beyond satisfying our bodily hunger. The dishes become an offering to community, the variety of foods representing the differences in gifts we bring to the table. Our extended family had a popular potluck of baked potatoes, all the adults bringing items we could use to dress up our spuds, similar to a taco night that likewise proved popular. It was interesting to see what items appeared on the table.

Of course, there are other adventures endemic to potlucks. Someone goes to a church picnic and experiences a bit of diarrhea or a stomach ache the following day. Was it the potato salad left on the picnic table too long? Anytime there are serving spoons handled by many hands in many bowls of food on the table, or temperatures cool, the food is ripe for bacteria even if we have blankets like tea cozies that bundle up our crock pots to keep them warm as long as possible, or coolers for dairy products and meat.

But food poisoning can occur whether one person or many are cooking and whether the pot is hot or tepid. I used to assume that meat was the culprit if food poisoning occurred, but other foods, like vegetables, can also harbor bacteria, as we have learned in discoveries of contaminated spinach and peanut butter.

Food allergies and dietary preferences are ubiquitous, but people don't always list the ingredients in their dishes. Someone forgets there is gluten in their salad and causes another person's illness. Sometimes, though, people are considerate and knowledgeable about such things. Before a recent church supper, a woman announced what items were being served: "We have pasta with meat, vegetarian pasta, and gluten-free pasta. Accidentally we briefly put the spoon from the pasta into the gluten-free dish. Please be aware." Eating with a crowd can be a tricky business, especially when there have been many cooks.

For years I have entertained groups of diners, usually no more than twenty-five people at a time, not an inordinately large group. I don't expect people to bring food, though they often do, providing a potluck feel to the occasion. Recently, I planned a holiday menu and buffet for approximately twenty friends. I made a few salads ahead of time and two Mexican spicy meat dishes in crock pots, while condiments, tortillas, bread, cheeses, fruit, and nuts rounded out the meal, and then I made some desserts to top it off. In addition to water, beverages were white and red wine and soft drinks. Except for the appetizers, I served the food once most of the guests had arrived. I had a wonderful time.

The next day I discovered one guest did not have a wonderful time but called an ambulance because she was very sick with an upset stomach during the night and couldn't keep any food down. I waited to hear the dreaded news that other guests had become ill, but only she went to the hospital. I wondered if she had a food allergy from some spice or herb she had not eaten before? I was sorry she went to the hospital alone.

We called her and visited her in the hospital. She had experienced food poisoning prior to this occasion and thought she had it again. One of the doctors we knew at the hospital informed us there was a flu virus going around that quickly made people sick to their stomachs. After a week, she was released from the hospital. I still don't know what made her sick, but I know that however careful we are with food safety and hygiene, eating—and particularly eating others' food—still has its risks.

The Bible has a few amusing passages about the Israelites wandering in the wilderness and complaining because they were afraid they wouldn't have anything to eat. The manna that God sent them came with some rules and instructions. The first time it dropped from the heavens, God told the Israelites not to keep it until morning. However, some of them did and, "it was full of maggots and began to smell" (Exodus 16: 20). However, on the day before the Sabbath, they were told to gather two days' worth because there would be no manna on the Sabbath; and it did not spoil. That must have been as puzzling to them as our spoilage is to us. The hummus may last a few weeks in the refrigerator while the olives soaked in brine develop mold. More significantly, the spinach may have come to a store with bacteria causing illness, while the romaine purchased at the same store grown in the same region of the country is safe to eat.

While it must have been fascinating initially to receive manna from heaven, after forty years the novelty wore off, and the Israelites again started to whine, remembering the fish, cucumbers, melons, leeks, onions, and garlic they ate in Egypt, and especially the meat.

The Lord says something like, "I'll give them meat!" "You will not eat it for just one day or two or five, ten or twenty days, but for a whole month—until it comes out of your nostrils and you loathe it—because you have rejected the Lord." And as the Lord promised, the wind brought in large amounts of quail from the sea. And they gathered them up but "while the meat was still between their teeth and before it could be consumed, the anger of the Lord burned against the people, and he struck them with a severe plague" (Numbers 11:33.) Now that's quite an "unlucky" pot.

Dinners, feasts, and celebrations are ubiquitous in the Bible. Communal living, sharing, and eating together are common. The stories in Exodus and Numbers about maggot-spoiled manna and quail that became poisonous show how dependent the Israelites were on God and on living together in community. They had to trust the land

and God to live. These stories about leaving the meat out too long, eating too much of it, and when and how much manna to gather are familiar to us today. Certain foods must be refrigerated, the bread dough must rise and bake before it is eaten, and we cook our meat to a particular temperature to make sure it's properly done.

Food rules and customs protect us and keep us healthy. Food laws promise some safety. In the Biblical stories, food binds people together and carries the message of relationship and brokenness. Clearly, the Israelites were meant to associate their food with their relationship with God and were advised against being careless about it. That they were ungrateful for what God had done for them and then disobedient and greedy had consequences. In their ungratefulness, they complained and were punished; driven by greed, they ate too much; and disobedient, they did not eat the food at the time they were instructed. The laws gave them identity; they may have seemed strict and arbitrary but breaking them alienated the people from God, and the results were illness and death. Keeping the laws bound the people together.

Adam Gopnick claims dietary restrictions are a big part of most religious practice, and religious leaders now "admit that the purpose of food laws is to create a form of symbolic solidarity that keeps a tribe or faith together."[23] Yes, "Do not work for food that spoils, but for food that endures to eternal life, which the Son of Man will give you" (John 6:27). When I read these stories, they do not seem quaint, and it isn't hard for me to see their contemporary relevance to the larger community of humanity.

Paul Roberts, Michael Pollan, and Wendell Berry, who know far more about our food supply than I do, write about how we grow our food, our depleted soil, the animals and the conditions in which we raise them, the lack of regulation, distribution, control of our food, and the Western and Standard American Diet (SAD). This diet in one of the richest countries in the world is unhealthy, taking out of the food the nutrients that preserve it only to add chemicals to replace what was taken out—a kind of example of a food disorder that contributes to malnourishment and poor health. Though our food industry feeds some people efficiently, it fails to ensure that everyone has enough to eat. In some ways, we seem concerned with controlling our food, and yet submissively we eat whatever stores and restaurants make available from agribusiness to us passive consumers. This takes a toll on our health, even when there is an abundance of food for some and malnutrition and hunger for others, especially seniors, children, and the poor.

In 2005, some 5 million people over age 60—about 11 percent of America's senior population—faced the threat of hunger, according to a study by the Meals on Wheels Association,[24] and the numbers are growing.

---

[23] (Gopnik 2011, 94)
[24] (Lieberman 2013, 13)

Many of these seniors, once part of the middle class, have seen their savings dwindle.

The gap between rich and poor occurs at tables. Lazarus eats the crumbs under the tables of the rich (Luke 16:21). When did that begin to happen here in the US where we produce so much food? Or has that gap always existed?

The film, *A Place at the Table* (2012), illustrates the problem of "food insecurity" by documenting the lives of children who don't have enough to eat. One little girl has trouble concentrating in school because of her hunger. When the teacher is talking, the girl imagines her as a piece of fruit. The film reports that one in four children don't know where their next meal is coming from and reminds us that acute hunger has devastating impacts on our health, our physical and mental development, and the economy. The surprising part of the film is the acknowledgment that we have the resources to ensure all people have enough to eat, but that our distribution and policies prevent that from happening, for example by allowing so-called food deserts.

Bridget Huber, a health and science writer, defines food deserts as "low-income census tracts where more than 500 people or 33 percent of the population live at least a mile from a supermarket that does at least $2 million in annual sales."[25] According to Orrin Williams, executive director of Chicago's Center for Urban Transformation, these areas "are often also cut off from bookstores, cultural or art institutions, where schools may be poor, and people may fear for their safety."[26] "Approximately 2.3 million US households live more than a mile from a supermarket and do not have access to a car. An additional 3.4 million households are one-half to 1 mile from a supermarket and lack transportation."[27]

The small neighborhood stores that do exist, often carry mainly or only snack foods short on nutrition and full of calories, and little or no fresh produce. Do people without transportation, living in these deserts, worry about food like the Israelites did in the desert?

The Obama administration pledged $400 million to eliminate these food deserts (Silva 2011, 151). One in six Americans faces hunger; 33 percent of American adults are obese, but obesity also may be related to eating processed foods from convenience stores—in food deserts. Thirty percent of food (or 96 billion pounds, according to Feeding America) produced in the US is wasted, according to the USDA. But if they can't access that food, surpluses of food do not necessarily help a billion people who go hungry (Fromartz 2011). Our food system has problems with access, distribution, the types of food we are eating, and food deserts—hardly lucky pots.

---

[25] (Huber 2011, 22)
[26] (Huber 2011, 24)
[27] (Silva 2011, 148)

While hunger has been discussed as a technical problem, some experts contend that, having identified how they will address food insecurity, governments should be held accountable. The Supplemental Nutrition Assistance Program (SNAP), designed to help families in distress by providing food stamps, is a program that works. The money spent goes directly into the food economy. More people, both from among the unemployed and those who are working, use it when the economy takes a downturn. So, how do we hold accountable ten US representatives who voted to cut food stamps while their own businesses received subsidies? One even quoted the Bible, "The one who is unwilling to work shall not eat" (Krugman 2013) (Pugh 2013). Olivier De Schutter, the UN's reporter on the right to food, says we view human services, including hunger, as negative rights, rather than as basic necessities (Lappé 2011)

Richard Le Mieux was successful in business and thanks to that, had a nice home, boats, and vehicles—until his business failed. Once he lost his material riches, friends and even his adult children dropped away. In *Breakfast at Sally's* (referring to the Salvation Army), he writes of his painful experiences begging for food. What is more humiliating is the cruelty of some of those who could most afford to help him, but let him know they thought he was a bum or worthless scum. One man refused him any money for a meal but was willing to pay Richard $400 for his little dog. The poor people with whom Richard became acquainted were often the most generous. If someone was given a twenty-dollar bill, they often shared it with others. The poor in this book know who really is "taking" society. They know about Wall Street too (Le Mieux 2009). Those who are hungry sometimes feel it is a matter of luck to find food when it should be a right. In Richard's heart-warming story, he finds community where people are eating together—at the Salvation Army.

While rising hunger and our reluctance to alleviate it is hard to swallow, other concerns about food, where it comes from, what's in it, and what happens to the land also require our attention. A recent article reports that since 1970 Americans have sprayed 1.8 million tons of glyphosate and other toxic chemicals in Round-Up, probable carcinogens, on crops, lawns, and gardens.[28] Its residue has been found on many foods including Cheerios. The vice president of Monsanto has denied that these products are carcinogens.

It's difficult to track down the sources of our food. While it appears we have many choices of food in the grocery stores, a few large monopolies of food corporations control the foods we purchase in the stores (Ebersole 2017). Sometimes it appears food drops into grocery stores from the heavens like manna, having been grown, as so much of our food is, on large industrial farms thousands of miles away from where it is bought and eaten. The costs of fuel to transport food and the additives to keep food fresh, colorful, and free from bugs

---

[28] (Ebersole 2017)

are reflected in the prices paid at the grocery stores, even though some of the additives diminish the nutritional value of the food. When most of us look at a pot of stew, we cannot determine where the carrots or onions were grown, or the meat raised, and we don't typically inquire. It's potluck, but is it lucky?

We are encouraged to eat locally and to know where our food comes from, but it's not always easy, and many reasons and excuses keep us from eating what grows where we live. The variety of foods we have come to expect would not be available if we ate only what is grown in our geographical areas. According to reports, a third of American households or forty-one million have gardens—up fourteen percent in 2009. Garden plots are also sprouting up in urban areas, though they are hardly widespread. (See the documentary *Food Patriot*).

For a long time, we've left growing food to others while we have become Wendell Berry's passive eaters, "victims" of whatever comes to the grocery stores and oblivious of the connection between our food and the land (Berry 1990, 146). His suggestion to grow at least one thing from planting to eating in order to see what it means to grow what we eat—to trust what we grow and eat—may not be practical for everyone in urban areas and because we no longer have the skills or knowledge for producing our food. What if we were to teach children to raise one food to share with their classmates or families?

Food, although sometimes referred to as simply a product or commodity, is part of a natural system in relationship with the soil. How the ground is tilled, fertilized, and the crops rotated determines the quality of the food grown. When the land is honored, the food is better. According to the experts, the present quality of the land and how food is raised leave much to be desired. Fertilizers, pesticides, and toxic chemicals kill bees and butterflies. Fewer earthworms and soil organisms contribute to the fertility of the soil. We are drawing down the water table and depleting farmland. Forests are disappearing.

We are poisoning the place where we live. At the age of twenty, Sandra Steingraber was diagnosed with a kind of bladder cancer associated with chemical exposure. In her book *Living Downstream: An Ecologist's Personal Investigation of Cancer and the Environment*, she writes of the connection between bladder cancer and the synthetic chemicals called aromatic amines which have been known to cause bladder cancer for at least 100 years. Their production has not stopped. Farmers who use imazethapyr, a pesticide that came on the market in 1989, also have elevated bladder cancer rates. Studies claiming that only 6 percent of cancers are environmental are blatantly out of date. Billions of gallons of fresh water that is turned into toxic fracking fluid cannot be made potable again (Drouillard 2012, 42) (Steingraber 2011, 22-25). How are we to live if we waste and poison our water?

Ask three hundred thousand West Virginians whose water was chemically contaminated in January of 2014 and who were told not to drink, cook, wash, or bathe with their tap water. For some time, anti-regulation politicians have spread their poisonous message to West Virginia, where funding for the Department of Environmental Protection has been cut at precisely the time the state government badly needs to hold coal and other energy companies accountable for the damage they are doing to our common environment. As people hauled fresh water to their homes from far away, one woman compared her family's situation to that in third world countries (Osnos 2014).

Droughts in some areas have already caused water to become scarce. Competition over these scarce resources impacts how much water goes to agriculture which produces hay, corn, and wheat for animals and processed food, and how much goes to producing food for people.

The soil is also depleted. Farmers often don't wait for the soil to renew itself through spreading manure, rotating crops, and allowing land to lay fallow, because low prices, the market, and agribusinesses pressure them to produce more and faster. Paul Roberts (Roberts 2008, 196) reports that growers are rushing to plant and re-plant their land regardless of whether the fields are ready for another planting because of markets' demands to keep customers buying more of what their fields are producing. Offering two for the price of one to encourage buying more than we need is common, and those items often contribute to obesity. Of course, that encourages greed—the same greed the Israelites had for a variety of food, and meat. An example of greed is meat portions on our plates averaging around nine ounces (255 grams) a day, four times the federal recommendation for protein (Roberts 2008, 207). Note: Recommended daily allowance (RDA) average for adults: 46 grams for women, for men fifty-six.

Michael Pollan, author of *In Defense of Food*, writes about the western diet, a diet of large portions, many calories, and less nutrition than many other diets in the world. He says, "we've asked for more and portions have ballooned with high-fructose, and refined grains—quantity rather than quality—resulting in people, both overfed and undernourished."[29] Once we're overfed and undernourished, we spend money on medications to cure us of what and how we have eaten. We have large, fast pots of food, but are they lucky?

Our animals, also on the western diet and eating large quantities of grain rather than grass, often spend their days in large feedlots. The dairy community in which I live is picturesque with cows grazing in green fields in the shadow of Mt. Baker; a few farms with many cows gathered closely together stand in their own excrement. Even though these large farms can produce more milk and meat at a cheaper price, more people are insisting that the animals they consume be raised humanely. This concern explains books with titles like, *The Ethical Meat Handbook* by Meredith Leigh and *Pig Tales: An Omnivore's Quest for Sustainable Meat* by Barry

---

[29] (Pollan 2008, 121-122)

Estabrook.

Much of the news about our food industry is discouraging and frightening. We read about (Roberts 2008) fewer calories expended growing food, less control over where it is produced, and fewer inspections for safety. Our food markets are full of fast, cheap foods grown in poorer soil with additives, more refined grains and sugars, and too much meat, say both Pollan and Roberts. (Ninety percent of the grain we eat is in the form of dairy foods and meat. Because of the resources used and the amount of waste, raising beef is particularly inefficient.)

Roberts grimly claims that our land cannot sustain the food industry we have, and the rush to grow and make food available cheaply and fast has already resulted in dangerous outbreaks of contamination—dangerous because some common antibiotics can no longer protect us from resistant food-borne pathogens (Roberts 2008, 185). (Animals are fed antibiotics to prevent them from getting the illnesses they would get standing in such proximity to each other and in filthy conditions, making them grow bigger and faster. Their cramped conditions and consequent lack of exercise likewise speeds their fattening. Because we ingest these antibiotics in the meat we eat, we are also becoming resistant to them. They will no longer be effective when we need them for an illness of our own.) Playing fast and loose with antibiotics is not worth that price. Perhaps our pots of food only seem lucky because for some people there is so much cheap food readily available.

Can we trust our food industry? Will these authors' reports be the impetus for changes in the way we grow and eat food? More importantly, can we take control to develop better methods to feed large numbers of people in healthy ways?

Some reports are positive. Signs of food resilience are cropping up around the country. More people are gardening; farmers' markets are popular, and the number of markets is increasing. In 2012 the National Farmers Market Directory listed 7,864, a 9.6 percent increase since 2011. Community Supported Agriculture (CSAs) groups and church communities are coming together to grow food on their lands (Ayres 2013).

My parents had a large garden when I was growing up. Mom canned the vegetables she raised and also some beef and salmon. Later she packaged some foods for a freezer. From "farm to table," "plot to plate," were not modern clichés but how food was grown, eaten, and preserved back then, or as Gabrielle Hamilton writes, in a time "when we didn't crow all over town about our artisanal, local, organic fwa fwa."[30]

After working in a city for years, I now live close to where I grew up, and have stopped at a farm not far from where my parents lived that sells eggs from chickens that are pasture-fed. I can see the hens running and

---

[30] (Hamilton 2011, 242)

pecking in a field.

The first time I stopped for eggs I was surprised that no one seemed to be available. The sign indicated the refrigerator in a porch enclosure close to the back door of the chicken farmer's house. Fortunately, I had the right change for a dozen eggs. An arrow directed me to another sign; please contribute twenty-five more cents if you are Canadian. I left my money in a container and was on my way. I doubt that anyone watched me from a window. They trusted me around food! It reminded me of how my father made material exchanges long ago: I'll do some work for you in return for a side of beef.

Gabrielle Hamilton in *Blood, Bones, and Butter* writes about her mother going to a farmer's dairy and picking up four gallons of milk and leaving the money in an honor system coffee can (Hamilton 2011, 23). The farmer trusted her. But if we can't stop along the road for local milk or vegetables, I want to trust that good food is still grown and raised, even if it comes from large industrial farms. We need to know about our water, soil, and food, and how they are connected, like the foods melding in a pot and becoming a stew. We need to keep learning how best to sustain our planet, provide food for the hungry, and keep ourselves healthy. We are all in this together, sharing air, water, and soil.

Food justice means bringing good gifts to the table, our knowledge, principles, and rules, and the best food to share at the potluck. Adam Gopnik says, "The way we eat is not a symbol of natural order but a community of belief."[31] Keeping Kosher knit a Jewish community together, just as hunger and manna sustained the Israelites in the wilderness. In our global economy, ideally, our identity can be found in a melting pot of good food for everyone, just as we have eaten others' ethnic dishes for so long we think of them as our own. I want to believe in that type of community.

I bought vegetables last summer from two farmers. I watched them pick Swiss chard and tomatoes and pull beets from their patches. After I washed the dirt off the fresh vegetables, we beheld their gorgeous colors. When we ate them, I thought of the faces of the farmers and their gardens and felt quite fortunate to be in a renewed relationship to the land. It's a small start. One of the farmers gave me some free rainbow Swiss Chard, because I had never tasted it fresh from a garden. The other farmer said it wasn't necessary for me to call each time I was going to stop by, that it didn't matter if we came while they were away and showed me where the money container was. I asked him if any of his produce had ever been stolen. No, he didn't think so, though another item had been taken—a scale to weigh the vegetables, a very precise scale that weighed small items like cherry tomatoes—and marijuana. But that one crime didn't keep him from trusting the rest of us.

---

[31] (Gopnik 2011, 110)

"Good food is like music you can taste, color you can smell! There is excellence all around you. You need only be aware to stop and savor it. "*Ratatouille*"—Chef Auguste Gusteau

Ratatouille

1 medium eggplant, ends cut off, and cut into chunks
1 large onion, chopped
2 peppers, 1 green and the other red, remove stem and seeds, and cut into pieces
2 medium zucchinis, ends cut off, and cut into pieces
6 garlic cloves, peeled
1 teaspoon dried thyme or 1 tablespoon fresh
2 medium or large tomatoes, cut into eighths
¼ cup olive oil
Salt and pepper

1. Heat oven to 400 degrees.
2. Mix all ingredients together.
3. Place in a large roasting pan or baking sheet, and salt and pepper to taste, and bake.
4. After 20 minutes, stir up the vegetables and cook ten more minutes.
5. Serve warm or at room temperature. Add ripe olives if you'd like. It's delicious with any kind of meat or sprinkled with some shredded parmesan cheese. It's also good tossed with pasta.

NOTE: I love this versatile dish, which can be cooked in a pot on the stove after browning the vegetables in the oil, as well as baked or roasted. When roasting, make sure the pieces of vegetables are about the same sizes, so they are ready at the same time. If you cook it on the stove, the ratatouille will be juicier, and you may want to mash the mixture a little.

Prayer:
Lord, thank you that we can come together to share and depend on each other for food. Forgive our passivity and help us respect the air, land, and water, and keep our food safe. Help us ensure that others have enough, and that we may have the will to use the methods that will improve how we grow and share food.

WAITING, RECEIVING, SERVING: Food's Language

"Epitaph for a dead waiter: God finally caught his eye."
—George S. Kaufman, playwright for the New York Times from 1917-1930

16

My father's side extended family circa 1950s.

Martha and Mary

Both serving food and being served ourselves are part of a relationship about hospitality. When Jesus visited the sisters Martha and Mary (Luke 10:38-42), Mary sat at Jesus' feet. Martha was the one who prepared food for their guest, which I would like to think included stew, some couscous, and yogurt.

    I feel bad for Martha when she complains about doing all the work without Mary's help, and Jesus tells her that only one thing is needed, and that what Mary is doing will not be taken from her. I want to say, "But Jesus, with more hands the work could be finished quickly, and we could *all* sit at your feet." And I want to add,

"Eating is important too. We can't live on spiritual food alone."

At various times we have all been Marthas and Marys. We've been slaving in the kitchen (even if we like doing that) while someone who should be helping us is in a good conversation, and we are missing out. The opposite happens when we are invited out. We are the ones being entertained even if we bring something to share—as we should. We all benefit by taking turns at serving and being served. When Jesus left Mary and Martha's home, perhaps Mary did the dishes while Martha put her feet up—hard as that is to imagine.

I like to think that Martha and Mary can change roles, and even if not, that hospitality was given and received. Jesus is served by having Mary's attention; Mary is served by her attentiveness to Jesus.

Hospitality entails waiting on others and graciously accepting the service of others, even where that service entails payment, such as at a restaurant. Perhaps that was Martha's mistake. Perhaps she thought that balance, fairness, or the equality of the exchange was amiss, when hospitality in relationship surpasses the way we calculate and figure.

I hope you are served by the following experiences about serving and being served.

17

Serving Food

People ask me: why do you write about food, and eating and drinking? Why don't you write about the struggle for power and security, and about love, the way the others do? The easiest answer is to say that, like most other humans, I am hungry.

—MFK Fisher

I don't delude myself. My only experience waiting on tables in the college campus dining room in Michigan wasn't anything like waitressing in a real restaurant. To this day, I can't imagine doing many things at once, remembering drink orders, who wants fries with that, all the while balancing heavy trays through a sea of hungry, often boisterous, diners.

After my experience serving family-style dinners during my second year of college, I knew I'd starve if I had to earn my degree waiting on tables in actual restaurants and vowed never to set foot in a restaurant except to eat.

You may be wondering what I was doing waitressing in a college food service. Today students have a smorgasbord of delights in dining rooms with cafeteria lines and ample choices like roast beef with mashed potatoes and gravy and lasagna with garlic bread. They have stations where they can make up salads with all the fixings, prepare tacos and enchiladas, or fill their cones with soft serve ice cream. They can sit at a table with their friends and eat it all. They didn't have Dean Hastings.

Dean Hastings thought young men and women should come together over dinner, maybe have some conversation, find they had something in common, and voilà! —a spark would ignite a relationship. Marriage would follow. He wanted students to eat family style. In family-style, people sit at a table, and bowls of food are served and passed among the diners. But family style leaves something to be desired. The contrived seating arrangement we had to endure to eat our dinners dampened our spirits and subverted the Dean's intentions.

First, we dressed for dinner. (I remember a sleeveless light pink woolen dress I wore once and stained. In Michigan, who wears a sleeveless woolen garment in the winter?) The women entered the east door of the dining room and walked to tables that sat eight. We stood behind every other chair, leaving an empty chair beside each woman, and waited. Meanwhile, the men came in through the west door of the dining room. They did not go to the tables until all of the women were in place, and all the men were crammed in the entryway behind a thick burgundy-colored velvet rope. I remember seeing them—the men—crowded together like cattle ready to be released into the field. They looked eager, perhaps calculating which tables they would go to, or perhaps they were just hungry. When all the women were at their chairs, someone unhooked the rope, and the men walked to the available chairs where we sat—boy, girl, boy, girl—and endured some uncomfortable dinners.

How did we liberated students of the '60s tolerate it? We must have been very hungry. I don't know if family style meals resulted in any lasting romances, or just indigestion. Our attempts to make conversation were awkward. I don't remember what we talked about. I don't remember making any new friends while dining. I was two thousand miles away from home and lonely. I already had a boyfriend I loved who lived off campus and ate elsewhere.

But when I waited on tables, I was too busy to be lonely. Waitresses were assigned either two or three tables for the evening. Fortunately, we were rotated so no waitress had three tables every evening, which would have made for an exceptionally busy night of waitressing. But even when we did have three tables, the students sitting at them could make the difference between keeping the platters of food coming while still hot and lagging behind and facing hungry and disgruntled diners.

One of the students that we waitresses dreaded having at our table, especially if we had three tables, was

Mike. He was a strapping hulk and a sports god of some kind with a strong jaw, wide nose with horned-rimmed glasses resting on it, a determined look, and an appetite that matched his size.

One night when I delivered the food to the table where he was sitting, he said, "Looks like shit," as though I was responsible for it. I only served the food. I was not personally attached to it. Not all of Saga Foods' meals were equally good. We said about Saga, *"Yours is not to reason why. Yours is but to eat and die."*

One evening I had three tables and Mike. I managed to keep up throughout the meal, or so I thought, until dessert. I didn't realize how important dessert was to him until on a run to the kitchen I found him in the kitchen taking plates of cake from the metal shelves of the food trays to his table. I didn't stop him.

Another student that increased our workload was a girl I'll call Kelly Motman. At the time, I didn't know the name of her condition. At family style dinners, she often sat alone and didn't converse with anyone. Maybe some supervisor allowed her to eat apart from us and our awkwardness. She consumed large amounts of food like Mike; only she was pale and thin with protruding cheekbones. By the time she'd finished her meal, she had many empty glasses and dishes in front of her. Her clothes seemed large and hung loosely on her body. At a time when we wanted to be part of the crowd, Kelly was an anomaly, standing out in a somewhat homogeneous group of students. I was mildly curious then but more so now. I know the word for bulimia now but didn't back then. I wonder what happened to her. I find myself hoping that she is well, and others reached out to her with kindness and compassion. I was not one of them. She must have been lonely, maybe in a different way than I was. I still see her in the dining room as a reminder that we can be surrounded by people around a table and all kinds of food and feel that something is missing. She must have been hungry for more than food.

Even with three tables to serve, I preferred waitressing to sitting at a meal family style. Waiting tables kept me too busy to feel homesick. The pay gave me a little spending money, whether I had two or three tables. We didn't receive rewards like tips for good service, nor was our pay docked for mediocre service. Mostly I waited on tables because I was waiting—waiting for a dinner I could make and serve to my family, waiting to grow up like the rest of us eating family style.

Dean Hastings had good intentions. Meals around tables are more than just putting on a pair of jeans and grabbing a bite. In retrospect, family-style meals would have been more fun if they weren't mandatory or matchmaking, perhaps with some music, candlelight, a glass of Cabernet, and a choice of companions. Meals together at a table are about community, about giving and receiving food.

Family style meals did not continue at that college. Yet students continue to come together. They meet in classes, libraries, chapel, dorms, and going through the cafeteria line. We are hungry for good food and for each other.

People ask me: Why do I write about food and eating and drinking? I'm hungry too—for the food that brings us together around tables—for serving and receiving. Bill Swing, a bishop in California says, "There's a hunger beyond food that's expressed in food, and that's why feeding is always a kind of miracle. It speaks to a bigger desire."[32]

Simple Tostadas

Serves 3-4

6 corn tortillas
1 15-ounce can of black beans, drained and rinsed
1 onion, chopped
2 cloves of garlic, chopped
1 bell pepper, green or red, chopped
1 15-ounce can of diced tomatoes, or use a couple of fresh tomatoes
Fresh shredded lettuce
2 cups shredded cheddar cheese
1 avocado, sliced
More fresh tomato, if desired
Sliced black ripe olives, (optional)
Salsa

1. Preheat the oven to 350. Sauté the onion for a few minutes and add the garlic. Sauté for a minute. Add the chopped pepper and cook another few minutes and then add the tomatoes, stirring to blend and the beans. Cook mixture for 5 minutes.
2. Sprinkle water on the tortillas and a little garlic salt. Spread them out on a cookie sheet and heat in the oven until crispy, about 5-7 minutes. If you prefer soft tortillas, heat them in the microwave about a minute. (They will be pliable and easy to roll up.)
3. When the tortillas are crispy, remove them from the oven. Slather on the bean mixture, and then lettuce, tomatoes, olives, cheese, and avocado. Top with salsa, and yogurt or sour cream if desired.

Prayer:
Lord, we want to be served. Help us to serve others what they need, even when we are strangers and not comfortable together. We are hungry for more than food. Teach us the gift of hospitality, and how to receive gifts from others graciously.

---

[32] (Miles 2007)

18

The Table

The world begins at a kitchen table...It is here that children are given instructions on what it means to be human.

"Perhaps the World Ends Here"

—Joy Harjo[33]

You prepare a table before me in the presence of my enemies.

—Psalm 23:5

Grandma prepared good basic meals, serving them at a beautiful Duncan Phyfe table set with a white tablecloth and china. My sister and I sat with care on the striped ivory and burgundy upholstered chairs—more carefully

---
[33] (Harjo 1994)

than we sat on our washable stainless-steel chairs at home. Nor would we fight at Grandma's table the way we did at home over who would eat on a certain yellow Melmac plate.

Typically, we'd stay at Grandpa and Grandma's after participating in some late school activity when my parents didn't want to drive the seven miles into town to pick us up. My grandparents' house was clean and orderly, though I suppose that when my dad and his brothers were young, they were hooligans and made messes too, just like my sisters and me. At Grandpa and Grandma's table, orderliness prevailed, whether during meals or when I sat there doing homework. I remember Grandma helping me with my Latin there one time, and I remember being impressed that she knew a word that wasn't in my high school Latin book.

Grandma's breakfasts around the Duncan Phyfe table tasted better than the same foods I ate at home. Mush was transformed into oatmeal in the china bowl with sugar and cream, orange juice looked sunnier and more freshly squeezed, and an egg cup held a boiled egg—all so elegant. I lingered to soak in that elegance, eating as slowly as I dared without being late for my first class of the school day.

The atmosphere at the dining room table was inviting, and guests were often present at the table. As an elder in the church, Grandpa had visiting preachers and their families over for Sunday dinner after the morning service. Grandpa told us about a minister who had adopted a small boy from Korea, and when he came for one of his dinners, the little boy's eyes took in all the food. When the potatoes were passed, he slipped an extra in his pocket. Before coming to the United States, he had not been able to count on when he'd have his next meal. His father reminded the boy there would be more potatoes and more meals.

When Clay and I were married and lived near Grandpa and Grandma for a summer, we looked forward to inviting them to our place for dinner after enjoying so many dinners at their table. I planned to try a new chicken recipe called Poulet Poache or Drunk Chicken. At the time, I was experimenting and thought any meat would taste better with wine, so I used a little Sauterne to marinate the chicken.

Grandpa and Grandma did not drink alcohol, and out of respect for them whenever they came over their children hid the brandy in their locked closets and the beer far back in their refrigerators. I was sure they'd never know about the drunk chicken; it would simply have a divine flavor once the alcohol burned off.

I was right. Though my grandparents arrived early, the meat showed no evidence of its soaking in the wine. Grandpa carried in a bag of green beans fresh from their garden. With a twinkle in his eye, he told us he'd come early to make certain we weren't putting any wine in the chicken. I busied myself preparing the beans for dinner so Grandpa wouldn't see me laughing. (Now I wonder whether he wasn't the one laughing.)

After dinner, as we retired to the living room, I turned around to see our cat, Monk, jump up on one of our chairs. He moved his head slowly up to the surface of the table, and peering ahead, clamped his mouth quietly onto a mealy bean someone had left on their plate. We couldn't imagine him liking green beans; if we had served him beans in his bowl, he wouldn't have touched them. Perhaps from a cat's perspective, everything that came from our table and plates must be good and worth stealing—a little like me believing that any meat tasted better with wine. We didn't leave any of the Sauterne-flavored meat, or he presumably would have chosen it.

I don't remember much about how things tasted, even the drunk chicken, or what we had for dessert. What I remember is simply my grandparents' company, that we'd made a meal for them, and how much we loved them.

Hand in hand with that memory is the overwhelming sense that my grandparents never ate anything hurriedly, not when we were with them, and not when they were alone. They were clear that food is more than survival, that it's community and nurturance. As Rachel Marie Stone writes, "Better the occasional meal shared with friends at McDonald's than organic salad in bitter isolation."[34] Meals were an occasion to converse with someone, whether family or friends or preachers. We didn't eat alone or in front of the TV or hurry to get on to the next thing. I try to keep alive the tradition of taking time to eat, but the experience of eating with family or friends over a leisurely meal may occur more in restaurants than around tables in our homes these days.

The truth is, when I have people over I'm not at leisure until the meal is nearly over and we're having dessert and coffee. I'm frazzled; my face is warm from the oven, or from fretting about everyone having what they need. Sometimes I hurry to get everything out on the table at one time, and I spill the gravy or drop a piece of meat. I've even forgotten to serve one of the dishes I made. I am a harried hostess. How did Grandma do it? And how did she and Grandpa foster such peace and such a sense of well-being around their Duncan Phyfe table that I remember it still?

Tables are alive with memories. Early in our marriage, Clay made an oak trestle table. We read newspapers, studied for exams, and shared many good meals and conversations around that sturdy and beautiful table. We still do. The grain in the oak boards seems to move in golden stripes the length of the table, its beauty revivified each time it is oiled.

Sometimes when the air is dry, spaces between the wooden boards open up ever so slightly and close when the air is more humid, as though they are breathing. A small cedar table, formerly a picnic table made by my father and modified by Clay, is also "alive" as a place of sharing meals.

Just such an alive table changed Sara Miles from being an indifferent secular restaurant cook and writer to

---

[34] (Weaver-Zercher 2013)

feeding the hungry at a church table. When Miles, who wrote *Take This Bread*, walked into St. Gregory's Episcopal Church in San Francisco, she came to the table which occupies the central place in the church, and stood with others around it waiting to take bread and wine (Miles 2007).

At tables, lives change. The character of Sister Helen Prejean in the film version of her 1993 book, *Dead Man Walking*, recounts a dream of reconciliation— of the victims, their families, and the murderers all dining at the same table. Some things can only happen in dreams. If the people affected by that tragedy had eaten together around a table, could they have enjoyed food without indigestion or even violence? Prejean would have been familiar with Psalm 23:5. "You prepare a table before me in the presence of my enemies."

What can we expect from sitting together at tables? Certainly, it is one of the few places at which we come face to face with others, feeding our bodies and our relationships. Adam Gopnik wrote in *The Table Comes First*, "Very different people do dine together, or try to. Good things do happen when people sit down for dinner."[35] Tables can be sites of peace and reconciliation, especially when food's involved. They offer proximity and nurturing possibilities that few other ordinary places do.

In the 2010 French film, *Of Gods and Men,* based on a true story, monks at the monastery of Tibhirine live harmoniously in a community with Muslims until the violence of the Algerian civil war breaks out. The monks disagree about whether to stay or flee. In the end, they decide to stay, attempting to live peacefully and without violence in their community. With imminent death looming, they have a Lord's Supper at a table, recalling Jesus' last supper and betrayal. As each monk tastes the bread and drinks wine, they smile, taking pleasure in the sacred moment. We touch each other at the Lord's Supper where the bread and our lives are broken, and we come together.

In the 1990 film, *Avalon,* Jewish immigrants in Baltimore, Maryland share meals and lively discussions at a large table. The parents clash with their children who are assimilating into the culture and treating the old traditions casually. At the end of the movie, the camera pans to a family table, empty, now small without its extensions, and adorned with a bouquet, while the family eats on TV trays facing a television set. Would the sad shot be less so if they were sitting at their table talking with each other without the television? Joy Harjo says in her poem, "Perhaps the world will end at the kitchen table, while we are laughing and crying, eating of the last sweet bite."[36]

---

[35] (Gopnik 2011, 250-251)
[36] (Harjo 1994)

Poulet Poache
"Drunk Chicken"
Serves 4

2 medium carrots
2 medium onions
2 celery stalks
6 tablespoons butter at room temperature
1 bay leaf
3½ lbs. chicken
2½ cups chicken broth
¼ teaspoon tarragon
1 cup Sauterne
12 ounces cooked wide noodles (whole grain if possible)
5 tbsp. flour
1 cup of half and half
6 tbsp. grated Swiss cheese

1. Slice vegetables very thinly and sauté in 2 tbsp. butter. Add ½ cup chicken broth with the bay leaf and simmer for 10 minutes.
2. Layer chicken in a skillet and add tarragon. Put the vegetables on top and pour in the Sauterne. 3. Add remaining chicken broth until chicken and vegetables are almost immersed. Cover skillet and simmer gently for about 30 minutes.
4. Remove the skin if you've used chicken with skin and bones, cut it into serving-size pieces, and arrange it on top of cooked wide noodles.
5. Cook liquid till reduced to about two cups. Prepare a roux by mixing flour with 4 tbsp. of butter, and cook gently for 2 minutes. Remove and cool.
6. Add to chicken stock and whisk. Boil, stirring for a minute. Add the half and half. Heat and pour sauce over chicken, fold in vegetables, and add cheese. Reheat if necessary.

Prayer:
Lord, thank you for the gift of coming together and dining face to face at tables where we talk, laugh, cry, eat, remember, and live.

19

Waiting on Diners

"Hello, I'm Darrin, your waiter, and food god."
—A waiter in Lansing, Michigan

The serving of food has drifted from the formal to the casual. Some restaurants may require men to wear ties and jackets before they bite into their rib eye steaks, but I have noticed most establishments are glad to take our money when we wear blue jeans. Typically, I don't see dress codes posted with the specials, and restaurant staff seem relaxed even when they are very busy. Not so long ago, formality was more common.

When my husband and I were at a conference in the "Big Easy," long before Hurricane Katrina, we had planned to eat at Brennan's, the famous French Quarter eatery. We called it "Brennan's for Breakfast," because the morning brunch includes the Bananas Foster, Eggs Benedict, and other breakfast treats that made them famous. We had a schedule conflict since our morning sessions began early, making a leisurely breakfast at Brennan's unlikely. We made reservations for dinner instead.

When we arrived and were seated at our table, our waiter, clad in a fancy white shirt and black pants, came to take our order. All the waiters were dressed alike and carried their trays to and fro formally. We could hear ourselves talk but were careful not to laugh too loud lest we disturb the other quiet diners. Televisions showing the New Orleans news or the Saints playing were nowhere in sight. It was quiet, awkwardly quiet. But then just as we were about to begin our soup, we heard a loud crash near us, and small pieces of broken glass flew in all directions. A few seconds went by as the glass settled on the floor, and the other diners took in the scene of the waiter and his tray that had unceremoniously slipped from his grip. And then laughter. The ice had been broken. After the crash, everyone seemed to talk a bit louder and laugh more freely. Better that the waiter dropped his tray than try to save it. I could imagine the tray teetering back and forth as he tried to recover equilibrium while the food and drinks flew down the back of someone's low-necked evening dress. No, better that he let the platter fall to the floor.

One of my friends went to a very formal high school academy away from her home. She tells about a similar dining incident. A young man waiting on tables in the dining room carried in a large tray of food and was about to slip. But rather than allow the tray to clatter to the floor, he broke his wrist to avoid the shame of a crash and spill.

Wait staff today are more casual and knowledgeable, often remembering lists of food items specific customers order without writing them on a tablet. A waiter once informed our table of diners what was available tonight and how each item would be cooked. When he finally finished what seemed like five minutes of a list of mouth-watering foods and how they would be cooked, I asked how we were to remember all the offerings. His response was, oh, you don't have to remember them all—only what you want to eat.

While a chatty waiter or waitress is unwelcome at an important business lunch or dinner, in many other settings the gratuities waiters and waitresses receive are related to the rapport they form with their customers. Wait staff, most of them female, are grossly underpaid and rely on tips (Jayaraman 2017). Restaurant workers hope to increase their pay, and one man with several fine-dining restaurants increased the hourly pay and began a merit-based system based on technical skills and hospitality in hopes of giving workers a living wage (Lappé,

Danny Meyer Has a Few 'Tips' of His Own 2017). Paying staff what they deserve may mean even more information wrapped up in mouth-watering words from the waiters. When I'm hungry (and more vulnerable), I'm susceptible to a "wait" relationship, and would want to know they are paid an adequate wage by the restaurant and tips too. (I only don't want to be asked if I'm still *working* on my meal. That simple word shifts the tone of the experience.)

I want to know the specials and what's good today. I have been steered away from a pasta dish by the advice of wait staff, even though they may not like pasta in any form, and nudged toward another of their favorites because they made it sound so delectable. Good staff sells a restaurant and its food. We sense that they enjoy the food and serving it too. If service is poor, a restaurant receives poor reviews.

A meal wouldn't be nearly so satisfactory if we couldn't trust our waiters and waitresses. If she broke down and cried, or worse, seemed angry, I'd likely leave the restaurant with indigestion. In the 2002 movie, *Mostly Martha*, a waiter returns to the kitchen several times to report to Chef Martha that according to a customer, the meat is not rare enough. In a moment of pique, Martha emerges from the kitchen, and much to the surprise of the customers, slaps a raw hunk of beef on the diner's plate. Some time ago, in reaction to the formality of dining, a hot dog diner in Chicago adopted the shtick of insulting its customers while they waited for their orders. Their ties, suits, and hairstyles were all on the chopping block in mock entertainment for their customers. It wouldn't have been my cup of tea. More to my liking is Adam Gopnik's remark, "We want chefs to give us not 'I work for you' but 'I feed you from love.'"[37] While we know their livelihood depends on serving us, we pretend chefs and wait staff are more to us than a business relationship, and we are more than their paycheck.

As wait staff and diners have become more casual and less formal, we can go too far in the bonds we form. I'm reminded of the cartoon I saw recently. A waiter, standing with other people eagerly looking on, stands by a couple seated at a table. The caption has the waiter saying something like, I'm Arthur, and I'm here to serve you. This is my family.

The other day a waiter said to me, "I'm Cecil, and I'll be taking care of you tonight." Taking care of *me*. I wanted to say, is that limited to this meal? Could you give me a little back rub? Perhaps some flowers? Pick my coat up from the Laundromat? Cecil, yes, I want to be pampered.

But now he is standing at the table of eager diners behind me, and I hear him say, "I'm Cecil, and I'll be taking care of you…"

No, Cecil, you are mine. You won't have time for them.

---

[37] (Gopnik 2011, 211)

Clay's Bananas Foster
Serves 2-4 depending on the portions

Clay watched a waiter carefully prepare this elegant dessert at our table in Ontario as we made our way from Toronto to Lansing, Michigan.

1. Peel and then slice 3-4 bananas lengthwise, and set aside.
2. Into a frying pan over medium heat, squeeze about half of a fresh lemon and melt a pat of butter.
3. Add bananas and a heaping tablespoon of brown sugar. Stir until sugar is dissolved.
4. Sprinkle 2 jiggers of dark rum over the fruit. Add 1 jigger of Triple Sec and 1 generous jigger of brandy.
5. Ignite the brandy mixture. Pour over soft vanilla ice cream.

Prayer:
Lord, thanks for all the people who wait on us and make dining out pleasurable. Help us to appreciate them in thought, words, and tips.

20

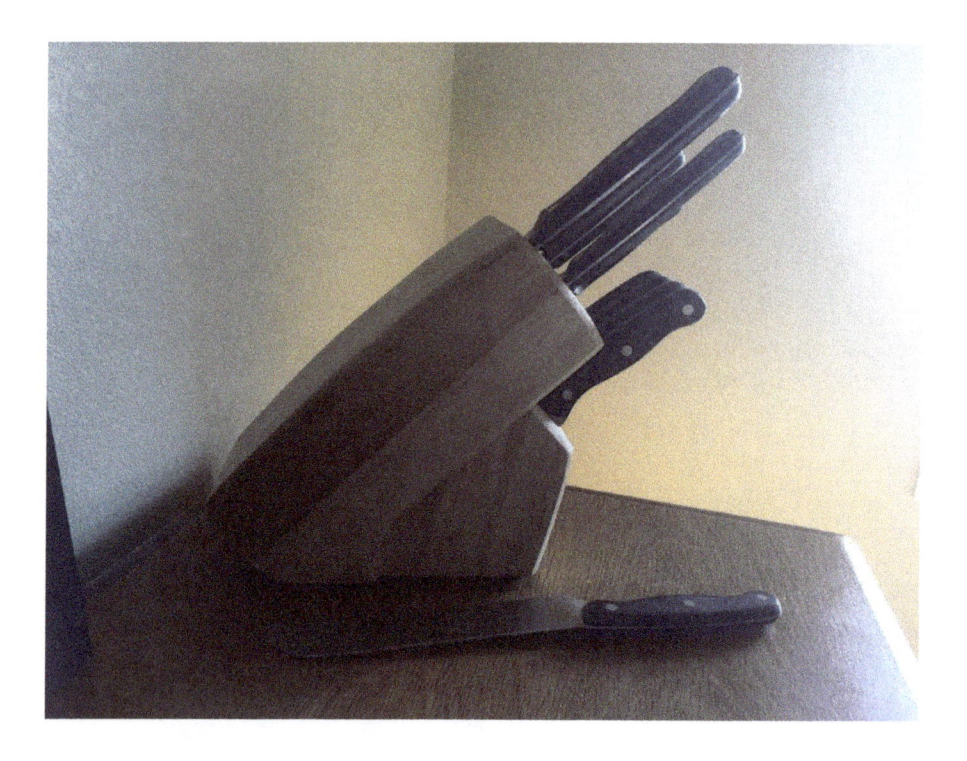

Food, a Language Insisting on Freedom

"I knew that with food and great hospitality perception can be changed easily, and that food is the only way to integrate society." [38]
—Ahmed Jama, a chef whose restaurant has been attacked by terrorists in Mogadishu, but who won't shut it down.

What is even better than eating out? Having someone make something for us to eat. A box of chocolates on Valentine's Day is great, but fixing me a whole meal? I'm in heaven, easily pleased. I come home after a busy day and walk into a kitchen with divine smells of roasted meat or vegetables. This is more than the red meat thrown on the grill, seasoned, seared, and fired. This dish consists of various ingredients like those found in recipes. I may *see* some dirty pots and pans on the cupboard, but I have not *touched* them. They are not dirty

---
[38] (Rice 2013, 33)

because of me; I haven't lifted a finger. And I can leave the kitchen to sit at a table and dine without thinking I will need to slave away in a hot kitchen after this luxurious meal. How special and pampered I feel, leaving the dirty dishes in the sink—unless it's one's husband who has cooked the dinner and expects some help in the kitchen after the meal, and, of course, then don't I badly want to help with the dishes?

When Clay and I were in graduate school, and both of us working while he was writing his dissertation, he took up cooking. There were no lessons. I think he just watched me or learned by hunger osmosis; when we're hungry enough for something more complicated than cold cuts, the cooking skills come. He talked about the bright colors the vegetables turn at a certain stage during a stir-fry, and his description elevated the dish from delectable to artistic. I know why so many artists' subjects are plates and bowls of fruits or vegetables. One night he made a chicken dish with a barbecue sauce so good we had to invite some guests to share it. He did not write down the recipe, and a few months later, could not remember all the ingredients or how he'd made it.

I love cooking too, only a little less than having someone make a meal for me. I'm a dunce when it comes to handy work like quilting, knitting, or crocheting, though I have always wanted to be able to give people gifts made with my own hands. One night at church, shortly before Christmas, I visited three stations set up to show us how to make nice Christmas decorations and gifts for the holidays. A young lady at the first station was making a centerpiece of evergreens and ribbons. Everything constructed seemed to need a glue gun that scared me since the gun resembled a curling iron, which had once burned a scar on my face. I did not want to be branded again.

The next station was a demonstration that involved making an ornament that we could take home. The instructor made it look easy, and no glue guns. I made an angel, but by the time I got it home, one wing was off and the other, well, this angel was not ascending or descending anywhere, even on the branches of our Christmas tree. I didn't even take it home for Clay to see.

Once again, I was down to the only gift I had—cooking and baking—and I told myself that food gifts like pumpkin or banana breads are appreciated as much as artsy crafty items. Who needs another feathery angel when cookies or quick breads are on the table?

Through my own fault, I only briefly enjoyed the luxury of having Clay prepare me a meal. One evening I worked late without notifying him. Unbeknownst to me, he had fixed an elegant dish, a layered soufflé with sauce poured on each layer, aptly called Tiered Omelet Mornay from the *Eet Smakelijk* cookbook. When I arrived home very hungry, he told me that the meal he had cooked had been ruined because I was late. A tiered soufflé with air beaten into egg whites does not stay fluffy long, and it had flattened. I was shocked at how much pride had gone into that soufflé. But it was delicious. I have never tried making it; I wanted to savor the recipe and remember it just as Clay had made it for our supper, knowing the soufflé or life could never be as good as that again. Meals made for famished people by someone they love are perfect even when the soufflé falls flat.

Recently, I read a story about a woman who stayed alone in one of those houses with a high-tech kitchen and all the latest equipment. While the owner was away, this live-in guest ate all the dinners in both the freezer and the cupboards of the house in which she was staying. She was out of food and hungry when a man stopped by for something stored in the attic. When he discovered how physically weak she was, he bought food and made dinner for her. While she was enjoying the delicious food, he said, "It's great to watch someone enjoying their food." She thinks she wants to make love with him, perhaps understandable after the sumptuous meal of couscous with a sauce of peppers, pine nuts, mushrooms, and pancetta, but after seeing she has regained her strength, he tells her he must go. Because of the meal, she finds the strength to land a job and restructure her life (Hadley 2013). Perhaps like you, I kept waiting for something to go terribly wrong in this story— the owner of the home would come home to find her cupboards bare and throw the woman out on the streets, or the man who bought food and cooked would attack the vulnerable woman. But nothing does. This is not always the case.

Those of us who live in luxury, safety, and comfort don't consider the task of making meals to be dangerous unless a stove blows up, or we miss the vegetables and chop on a finger instead of a veggie. Ahmed Jama, a family man, and chef who had a successful restaurant in London, left his life of safety and comfort there to return to cook in Somalia, where he was born. He continues to cook delicious food there even though his restaurant has been bombed. Not once but several times suicide bombers have blown themselves up at his restaurant, killing some of his employees. He himself has been threatened, hit with shrapnel, and singed from the heat of suicide bombers. Mangled bodies of employees and customers have been scraped off the restaurant walls. Al- Shabaab, an Islamist militant group, think he is a spy for the British government.

Only a passion for feeding and serving others can explain what he has endured (Rice 2013). Jama says. "Someone has to start somewhere in history to change a nation. I wanted to show what could be done, to make people forget about hunger and bloodshed, to learn to live with each other. I wanted to become a man of hope."[39] This belief that Jama can change lives with food gives new meaning to the food fights we have in comfortable settings, where the choices have to do with which foods to eat, the chemicals added, and not the life-threatening conditions under which they are eaten. I often think of Jama and pray that he is changing lives and not giving

---

[39] (Rice 2013, 30)

up his life while cooking his delicious meals and providing nourishment for others.

Because of a meal, the Biblical Jacob had to flee and find a new life in a foreign land. With help from his mother, Jacob snatched from his father Isaac what he thought was a blessing, a blessing intended for his other son, Esau. Their mother Rebecca, the accomplice, helped Jacob fool his blind old father Isaac by disguising himself as his brother Esau and serving Isaac a meal. And his suspicious father was willing to believe him after the good food (Jacob and Esau, Genesis 27). I wonder whether Jacob ever regretted that meal which fractured his relationship with his twin brother Esau while he grasped for blessings that he already had.

After years of not cooking, Clay is in the kitchen once more. The only danger in my kitchen is the way I brandish the knives, which seem to be sharper these days. Sometimes Clay takes the knife because it is too painful for him to watch me maneuvering it. The onion and peppers he cuts are in neat rows of perfect matchsticks, unlike mine. We work together. A stir-fry requires all our hands and commands of when to add the garlic and ginger and then the sauce, each of us glancing at the recipe while leaning over the stove. We step around each other finishing the dish. After the many meals I've made for Clay, he's forgiven me for being late that night long ago when he made the Tiered Omelet Mornay. Most of the time I make the meals, but he helps set tables and clean up (the worst job), and he sometimes wields the knives.

If Clay were to make meals for me again, I would begin to feel entitled somehow, deserving of such luxury as though it were a birthright, as though one had an inheritance and would feel entitled to more than food—that I was the blessed one.

Not many of us would give up a birthright to be fed a good meal, although hunger and enjoyment of food can lead to gratefulness so foolish it can change our lives.

Quick Fried Fish in Chinese Sauce

1 lb. fillet of white fish (e.g., sole, carp, halibut, cod)
½ teaspoon salt
2 tablespoon cornstarch
1½ tablespoon butter or olive oil
2 stalks scallions or ½ red onion, chopped
3 slices ginger root
2 tablespoon soy sauce, preferably low sodium
4 teaspoon wine vinegar
2 teaspoon brown sugar

Adria L. Libolt

2 tablespoon sherry or Chinese rice wine
2 tablespoon stock

1. Cut the fish into small thin pieces. Sprinkle and rub them with salt and cornstarch. Shake free any excess.
2. In a bowl, mix together the scallion or onion, ginger root, soy, vinegar, sugar, sherry, and stock. Set aside.
3. Heat the oil in a pan. When hot, remove from heat for 30 seconds and gently lower the fish into the oil, piece by piece. Return the pan to the heat and fry for 2 minutes. Remove fish and drain.
4. Heat the butter or oil in a frying pan. Pour in the sauce mixture and stir over high heat for 1 minute.
5. Add the pieces of fish, spreading them out over the pan. Turn and mix them with the sauce for 1 minute.
6. Remove with a slotted spoon and arrange them neatly on a heated platter. Pour the remaining sauce over the fish and serve. Serves 6-8.

Prayer:
Lord, thank you for feeding us and for those who generously make meals for others in comfort and safety. Keep Jamal and other cooks and chefs safe while they cook and feed people in war-torn areas.

21

Wildly Eating Each Other

"There are some who can live without wild things and some who cannot."
—Aldo Leopold
"These all look to you, to give them their food at the proper time."
—Psalm 104:27

Until recently, I was an urban animal feeder, not because I intended to fatten up creatures to eat them myself. We had always fed the birds and then, I fed squirrels—and other four-legged furry creatures that like cracked corn—though my intention was to limit the feeding to squirrels. I fed them because they loved a large tree (too close to the house) that had to be removed and because they respected my garden and didn't dig up my flowers. Mostly I fed them because they were hungry and because Clay built a ladder going up to the kitchen window with a tray at the top. All I did was open the kitchen window, pour cracked corn and some bird seed in the tin insert in the tray, and watch them nibble as I cooked or washed the dishes.

Sometimes the love of a pet generalizes to the appreciation of all animals. The boundaries blur between furry four-legged friends and less domesticated animals. Pets sometimes give us a touch of the "wild," depending on how crazy they are. One writer disagreed with that. He made a distinction between wild and domestic animals, calling the domestics, "goofy," after the Walt Disney dog. Parents at zoos remind their children that adorable lion cubs and small tigers are not like their cat Muffin, regardless of the resemblance. But the similarities are unmistakable, which is likely why we read too frequently about a well-meaning soul who takes in a wild animal that turns on them, harming or killing them or someone else. Even so, puppies and kittens are "wired" so they don't recognize they are living in someone's home and are not allowed to chew up slippers, bite the chair legs, or climb up the curtains. We "tame" puppies and kittens so they can live in our houses. I was amused when my cats from inside the house watched animals and birds as though they were a novelty with a vast difference between them.

I've heard all the reasons why feeding squirrels and other outside animals isn't a good idea. They may come to depend on the food and lose their instinct to survive on what nature provides them. And it's not as though squirrels are a dying breed, even though some starve in the winter. In my Michigan yard, they seemed to sustain themselves. Another reason for not feeding anything out there is the likelihood of attracting less desirable animals like raccoons and mice that may invade a warm house in the winter. I did indeed find that the food tray set out for squirrels became a magnet for other less welcome creatures.

One evening I walked through the kitchen in the dark and saw a large ominous ball of fur blocking my view out the small window. I tapped on the glass, and a raccoon looked up from the tray as though to say, yeah, I know you're there, so? I want to discriminate between those I intend to feed and those I don't, but raccoons are hungry and have babies to feed too. I wish they were more frightened of me, but I wouldn't tangle with one. Those teeth and claws could be vicious.

One night long before we had a tray for the squirrels, we saw raccoons on our birdfeeder. Clay thought he could outsmart them. The birds feed by day and the raccoons by night, so he took the top of the birdfeeder and placed it in the house. The next morning, I looked out the window, and since I didn't see the birdfeeder, I ran to Clay and told him the raccoons had taken the birdfeeder! He had a good laugh at my expense. I brought the squirrel tray in at night too, but often forgot, and sometimes the whole ladder toppled over from the weight of a raccoon.

I understand why we use "squirrely" to describe craziness. I've watched a squirrel chase another and then change position, so the chasee becomes the chaser. I've seen two squirrels approach each other and leap in the air as though they had not expected to see each other and scare themselves. I've seen them sleeping spread-eagled on the driveway. I have a picture of one resting on the seat of a bike in my backyard.

Yes, they are rodents. But with their fluffy tails, they don't look mousy. Initially, I thought they all looked alike. How did I know that different squirrels came to the feeder, and the same squirrel wasn't there all day pigging out? Okay, I spend too much time at my window watching the tray and the birdfeeders. But the squirrels do not all look alike, and their habits distinguish them. One faces the window and sometimes stands on hind legs with his front legs spread out, letting me know his gender. I call him Batman because of his position. Another has a small patch of fur missing on one side of its face. This one is Mange. The one with a nick out of her ear is Notch.

In some countries, like Nigeria, animals such as squirrels are on their own. People in other cultures often feast on animals that most of us don't eat. I read recently that most of the people of the world either eat meat or want to eat it. Restaurants in Nigeria that appear more like outdoor coffee shops with dirt floors display racks of small toasted squirrel-like animals called bush meat. Until I saw their eyes, they reminded me of a rack of jerky or leather flip-flops. Environmentalists say hunting and eating those animals isn't sound ecology because animals higher on the food chain need the "bush" meat and when the animals are removed, the animals smaller than bush meat and lower on the food chain have no predators. We know that in some cultures, people get their protein from animals we don't prefer to eat, like cats, dogs, horses, and whales. In China, especially during the winters, it is believed that eating dog meat keeps people warm. Dog and whale meat may taste fine, but we make cultural judgments based on squeamishness, how endangered the animal is, or how friendly we are with the protein.

When we stopped for lunch at a restaurant in Nigeria, one of our guides ate some of the bush meat and said it tasted like barbequed salmon. Perhaps. It wouldn't take much for me to become a vegetarian there. The meat looked too much like Batman, Mange, and Notch. Nigerians don't feast on fat juicy raccoons because they do not inhabit the country. Recently I've noticed the eyes of raccoons—dark and beautiful—and their ears like those of teddy bears. Naming animals and seeing their faces makes it difficult for me to eat them. Some people will not eat creatures with faces. In her memoir, *Blood, Bones, and Butter*, Gabriel Hamilton tells of confronting the chicken she was going to kill for dinner—perhaps something I could do if hungry enough if I didn't look in their eyes (Hamilton 2011, 61).

When my nephew was a small boy, he was fascinated with raccoons and had a collection of them, some ceramic, others stuffed toys, and one carved out of wood, all lined up on a shelf in his room. Joey and his family enjoyed a flock of ducks living by the creek which flowed by their backyard. One evening there was a massacre of the ducks. The next morning feathers littered the lawn. My nephew's parents speculated that the ambush was the work of raccoons. Soon, without a word, the collection of raccoons disappeared from Joey's shelf.

We don't want to see the viciousness of hunger in the dark or daylight. We know, but we look the other way. The pretty scene of ducks on a bubbling creek is illusory; hiding under the surface is the messiness of those eating others. When the world closes its eyes, other creatures like raccoons step out to claim their place and others' lives. Day and night we feed on each other.

Some people have suggested we should eat more wild animals, particularly those that have become pests and proliferate. Some non-native species that were brought into areas, either intentionally or accidentally, and have upset the balance of the habitat by their aggressive destruction of native plants and other species, are finding themselves, in our nose-to-tail society, on the menu (Bruni, Malicious but Delicious 2013). A site, "Eat the Invaders," suggests eating delicacies like Asian Carp, an invasive species of fish that threatens other fish and fishermen in boats in U.S. waters. Of course, some wild eaters (and chefs) go overboard with "wild" eating too. I feel a bit nauseous reading Dana Goodyear writing about eating "a Filipino *balut*—an unhatched duckling, cooked in its shell and eaten entire, beak, feathers, and bones."[40] Is it my cultural squeamishness? The title of her book, *Anything That Moves: Renegade Chefs, Fearless Eaters, and the Making of a New American Food Culture* supposedly describes elements of the food movement. But I couldn't get beyond the review of the book.

On a lovely day in October some years ago, Clay and I took our pontoon boat down the Grand River for one last ride before the winter chill set in. The trees were aflame in gold, reds, and oranges. Fish jumped from the calm water. Yes, Robert Browning's "God's in His heaven—All's right with the world," that type of day. As we rounded a bend, we saw the hunter's blind, and a man with a gun, and his soundless, unblinking decoys on the river. I wanted to protest that this dissonant scene did not fit into our day. But I eat meat; I've eaten duck. We were quiet as we returned the boat to the dock. Sometimes shortly after dusk, we hear the growl of raccoons competing for food, or the screech of the rabbit being devoured as other animals take the night. Even if we eat meat infrequently or as a condiment, our appetite for it prevents us from being too romantic. Sometimes we are hungry for an idyllic world; we don't want to see what we know.

By feeding birds and squirrels, I attracted raccoons. In a small way, I upset a balance in my yard when I tried to feed one wild species and not another. Like the raccoons who knock over the tray of food meant for the squirrels, we, without thinking about the consequences, often forget that we "knock over someone's food tray" because of our appetites. Much of our meat is domestic and raised to be eaten, but still harms the environment we all share. Whether we eat what's wild or domestic, we often don't consider the question of balance.

---

[40] (Epstein 2013, 66)

According to Paul Roberts (Roberts 2008, 209), ninety percent of the grain we eat is in the form of meat or dairy. This is grain that could be available to feed people directly. We could grow fruits, vegetables, seeds, and nuts instead of large crops of corn and soybeans for fast foods and for our animals. And although we are not likely to give up eating meat, it is not necessary or healthy to eat four times the federal recommendation for protein that we presently eat. We ought at least to chew on that.

Recipe? Except for wild salmon now and then, I don't cook rabbit, wild boar, venison or any other wild animal. But if I did, I'd brown it and cook it slowly with wine in a stew with lots of fresh herbs and vegetables as many recipes suggest.

One of my friends says, about the domestic variety, "So many cats. So few good recipes."

But all the talk of the wild has made me hungry instead for a good comforting meatless pasta.

Spaghetti, Cauliflower, Green Olives, and Almonds

1½ cups pitted brine-cured green olives (plain or stuffed)
½ cup chopped flat leaf parsley
½ cup olive oil
1 head cauliflower, cut into 1-inch wide florets (8 cups)
½ teaspoon salt
3 garlic cloves, chopped
½ teaspoon dried red pepper flakes
¼ cup water
¾ lb. spaghetti or linguine
½ cup Pecorino or Parmesan cheese
¾ cup whole almonds with skins, toasted and coarsely chopped

1. Pulse olives and parsley in a processor, then transfer to a bowl.
2. Heat oil in a skillet over medium heat until hot but not smoking, then cook the cauliflower in the salt, stirring occasionally until golden, about 8 minutes.
3. Add the garlic and pepper flakes, stirring occasionally until cauliflower is tender and the garlic golden, 3-5 minutes. Stir in ¼ cup water and boil 1 minute.
4. Add olive mixture and cook, stirring until heated through, about 2 minutes.
5. Cook pasta in 6-8 quarts of boiling salted water, stirring occasionally. Reserve 1 cup of water.
6. Drain pasta and return to pot.
7. Add cauliflower mixture and toss well, then add cheese and toss again. If the mixture is dry, moisten with cooking water.
8. Sprinkle pasta with almonds and serve with additional cheese on the side.

A Squirrel's Prayer

A squirrel eats seeds
left beneath the birds' table
Lazarus to their wealth
wanton waste its survival.

It wasn't brazen begging
but the ritual of resignation
taking where it's found
that gnawed at my guilt
until I laid

three slices of stale wheat bread
on the bird seed tray.
The squirrel climbs the large maple
to the window,
leaps to the sill
picks up two slices with sharp front claws
stands nibbling, turning the bread
kneading, a grateful rosary
Thank you for my daily bread.

Prayer:
Forgive our often wild plundering of your creation and the kind of hunger that consumes and keeps us from seeing what we know—that others sometimes suffer because of what we eat. Thank you for the beauty and wonder of other creatures.

MEMORIES AND ASSOCIATIONS—Coming of Age and Food Fighting

22

The Palate of Place

As a child, Chang-Rae Lee wanted the American food he saw his friends eating. His mother tried to prepare lasagna, fried chicken, and mashed potatoes—the sort of food families in New York were eating. He realized later that these foods were "much heavier and plainer" than his family's Korean food. They were foods "without association, unlinked to any past,"[41] for his family, but they fixed them to the unfamiliar place in which they now lived.

    As children, we form strong associations with certain foods. I did not live in another country where I was trying to assimilate, but certain foods of my youth stir up strong associations either because they were a staple I loved, like potatoes or milk, or because I associate an event with certain foods and consequently either like or

---

[41] (Lee 2011, 277)

avoid them.

Potatoes were for me a pleasurable part of my heritage and culture. Pasta, rice, quinoa, barley, or other grains, not so much. Potato salad was always on the picnic tables, and if Mom and Dad went out for dinner, Mom rewarded us for staying behind with homemade French fries before the sitter came. A staple in more than one country, the potato, like pasta in Italy, is one of the ultimate comfort foods whether baked, steamed, fried, or in salads. (When I was in Nigeria I learned a certain yam—different from our Yukon golds, russets, or sweet potatoes—is a basic food; the country boasts the "yam capital" of the world.)

Other foods, for reasons that are not always clear, we avoid. We see others eat and enjoy them, but they are not for us. I love most seafood but avoid mussels, not because of the taste but the texture—a little bumpy and snotty. I can eat hot dogs now, but after getting sick on one long ago, it took some time for me to overcome my disgust and try one again.

Some foods vividly recall events like, say, food fights. One of the incidents I write about below involves eggs, which I did not like until later in life. It reminds me of how some foods seemed plentiful, and as a child, how little I thought about wasting food. One report reveals that about half of the world's food goes to waste (Oxfam 2013, 3), a shocking statistic considering a report stating that some forty-six million Americans use food stamps on any day (1 in 7), many of them women and half of them children (Ratner 2012).

When strawberries ripen here in Washington, I regret wasting them. I remember how I used them like juicy weapons and threw them at other berry pickers in fights as we picked in berry fields for cash. One memorable skirmish left a few crimson stains without many other consequences unlike the fights over our food today, which have more serious ramifications for our health.

23

Food from Heaven

"I have friends who begin with pasta and friends who begin with rice, but whenever I fall in love, I begin with potatoes...I have made a lot of mistakes falling in love, and regretted most of them, but never the potatoes that went with them."

—Nora Ephron, *Heartburn*

When our Nigerian friend John came to visit our church to raise money for his ministry in Nigeria, he came for dinner. I don't remember what I fixed. It may have included mashed potatoes—the kind I make with garlic, either roasted or boiled with the spuds, and butter and milk or sour cream. During our dinner conversation, John told us a Nigerian meal was not a meal unless it included a pounded yam. He called it food from heaven. As he talked, I thought about manna, the food the Israelites depended on in the desert in Biblical times. But manna is described as wafers like some of those served at the Lord's Supper, so light they would melt on one's tongue and yet provide what the Israelites needed while wandering in the wilderness.

John's words took on new meaning when we visited Tiv land, the home of his tribe in Benue State, and pounded yam with egusi sauce became our chief sustenance for the trip. At Zaki Biam, we went to the largest yam market in the world. Their yam is also the largest I've seen, some of them like logs as long as two feet, with brown skin and shaped much like our Idaho potatoes with white flesh inside. We visited several Tiv communities where the women's fellowship from the church prepared and provided such yams. We heard Nigerian friends invite each other over by saying, "You'll have to come to my place for yam."

Women, often singing as they worked, cooked the yams on an open fire, then pounded them with a pestle in a big mortar. The stiff mixture was shaped into serving sizes of big balls that looked like bread or pie dough before it is rolled out. We soon learned to split the round in half, and even then we could not always finish one. We North Americans often were given utensils to pick up the starchy stiff yam, but I soon found it more practical and efficient to pinch off pieces from the ball to soak up the egusi, a spicy tomato sauce combined with a spinach-like green and ground melon seeds.

Like the Nigerians, some of us shaped the pieces like play dough into little cups to scoop up as much egusi as possible. The pounded yam is also good for soaking up the egusi sauce left on your fingers, and by the time I had finished my meal, my leftover yam round was marked with fingerprints of egusi sauce.

We often had chicken, too, cooked over an open fire, and sometimes a choice between yam and the rice that grew in this fruit capital of the state. Sometimes coleslaw was also served, and I couldn't resist its crunch with the soft yam, though John advised us to stick to cooked food. Sometimes for breakfast, we were served plantain fried like French fries along with eggs. Some of our team joked about yam and eggs and "I yam what I yam," as we traveled to the next community and another dinner of pounded yam. I wondered what yams or cooked pounded yam would be like in a food fight and whether any of the little kids in Nigeria threw them around.

Maybe not. I remembered reading before our trip that in many countries, people don't worry about what they like or don't like but whether their stomachs are full.

Like the Israelites, traveling across the desert with manna to eat, we had to depend on what we were served in a foreign land, and like the Israelites, we thought about variety. Maybe manna tasted like having pounded yam every day. Maybe they asked, "Are we having manna again for dinner? We know they asked for meat and ate quail. As for us, we talked about the coffee, pasta, hamburgers, and chocolate we would have when we returned to the States.

Once at home, I couldn't find the Nigerian food from heaven at any grocery store. Perhaps it's not practical to export the yams. I found the usual red yams and Yukon golds, and picked up the golds, maybe not food from heaven, but local. After I boiled them, I mashed them. If I'd not added the garlic and butter, they would have tasted a lot like pounded yam balls—food from heaven.

Mashed Potatoes

1. Cut 4 or 5 medium-sized potatoes into quarters and add to a pot of boiling water. New potatoes and Yukon golds have fairly thin skin, and I don't always peel them. Add at least 6 cloves of peeled garlic. (As an alternative, I've also roasted the garlic while the potatoes are cooking and added it at the time I mash the potatoes for an even richer garlic taste.) Add some salt to taste.
2. Boil them until tender, about 15-20 minutes. Test them with a fork to make certain they are soft.
3. Once the potatoes are cooked, drain them, reserving the water. Heat a little milk with butter. Mash the potatoes and garlic and slowly add the milk with the butter. Add some water and heat on the stove, but be careful because the potatoes will stick and burn quickly. If you need to re-heat them at the last minute, you may want to use the microwave instead.

If you are fortunate enough to have leftovers, take the cool potatoes and mix them with 1 egg, or 2 if you have a good amount of potatoes, and a little chopped green onion. Sauté a little more onion in a frying pan. Shape into patties and fry them. They are good alone or with bacon or ham for breakfast.

I've also used mashed potatoes as a crust for quiche-like dishes which you can simply fill with beaten egg and your favorite sautéed vegetables with some grated Swiss or Cheddar cheese on top.

The following "recipe" is adapted from Mark Bittman of the New York Times.

Note: I do not use precise measurements, just as I don't use precision in measurements when making white potato salad.

Yam Potato Salad

4 medium sweet potatoes (about 1½ pounds),
peeled and cut into 1-inch chunks. (Sometimes I use half white potatoes.)
1 large onion, preferably red, chopped
½ cup extra-virgin olive oil
Salt and freshly ground black pepper
1 to 2 tablespoons minced fresh hot chili, like jalapeño
1 clove garlic, peeled
Juice of 3 limes, or more if you like that citrusy flavor
2 cups cooked black beans; canned are ok if drained
1 red or yellow bell pepper, seeded and finely diced
1 cup chopped fresh cilantro

1. Heat oven to 400 degrees. Put sweet potatoes and onions on a large baking sheet, drizzle with 2 tablespoons oil, toss to coat and spread out in a single layer. Sprinkle with salt and pepper. Roast, turning occasionally until potatoes begin to brown on corners and are just tender inside, 30 to 40 minutes. Remove from oven; keep on pan until ready to mix with dressing.
2. Put chilies in a blender or mini food processor along with garlic, lime juice, remaining olive oil and a sprinkle of salt and pepper. Process until blended.
3. Put warm vegetables in a large bowl with beans and bell pepper; toss with dressing and cilantro. Taste and adjust seasoning if necessary. Serve warm or at room temperature, or refrigerate for up to a day.

24

One Potato, Two Potato: More on Potatoes

*and if we did not eat your strength,
you'd drive it up, into a flower.*

"In Praise of the Potato"
—David Williams, from *Traveling Mercies*

We were a meat and potatoes family. The casseroles Mom fixed on Saturday evenings were a change, but they often had potatoes in them too; "Whole Meal in One" had meat, rice, and potatoes held together with tomato soup. Potatoes grew well in northwest Washington State; variety in a meal was in the fixing—potatoes boiled, mashed, fried, scalloped, or roasted. Someone who shares my heritage once joked that if potatoes were not being served, it wasn't necessary to pray before the meal.

    The spud is part of my Dutch heritage. One meal, called "hutspot," not to be confused with c*hutzpah,* consisted of mashed potatoes and carrots. The orange color of the dish represents the Dutch Royal family. A variation called *stamppot* may include cabbage, brussels sprouts or sauerkraut, and smoked sausage or bacon.

My husband, who is half Dutch, claims that Dutch cuisine reaches its maximum excitement and spiciness when potatoes are mixed with carrots. Perhaps all the hot cuisines, Mexican, Thai, and barbeques have dulled our tongues. To be sure, food cooked in the Dutch immigrant communities in the Northwest was comfort food. The potato's distinguished history indicates it may always have been a comfort food and a survival food.

In the Netherlands, the story of the potato goes back to 1574. During the Eight Years' War, liberators breached the dikes of the lower lying polders surrounding Amsterdam and flushed out Spanish soldiers camping in the fields. Legend has it that the soldiers left bits of cooked potato behind. The Dutch must have fallen in love with those potato pieces.

Though the cuisine in the Netherlands is now cosmopolitan, the potato still has a central place on many menus. When I was there, sometimes I ordered an entrée with potatoes as my side and received an additional order of fries. Like bread served in France, potatoes are a side even if redundant. Surprisingly, I saw many tall, lean folks. Perhaps all that biking as a means of transportation keeps them from becoming couch potatoes.

One museum in Amsterdam has a famous painting featuring potatoes. Vincent Van Gogh's "The Potato Eaters" hangs in the Museum of his name, and no copy compares to it. The brown tones in the painting suggest that the family sitting around the table eating potatoes is nearly inseparable from the earth where they've dug up the potatoes for their sustenance. The people with their bulbous potato-shaped noses remind the viewer that they are what they eat.

Another, perhaps apocryphal, story in addition to the one about the potato's history, illustrates the importance of the potato in my tradition. At a regional church meeting, the women at the host church were serving the meal, but the entire meal was not ready. They served the meat first while everyone waited for their vegetables. The potatoes came, and after everyone had finished their meals, an elder stood up to "tank da vimmen." Then he added, "but da vimmen are not perfect. I'm reminded of a little 'moeder moppje'" (a story about a mother).

A mother was breastfeeding her baby in a park when another mother walked by with her young son. "Vhat is she doing?" he asked.

His mother said, "She is feeding her baby in the natural way."

"Vhat? He said, "all meat and no potatoes?"

Hutspot

3 medium-sized potatoes, peeled and cut into smaller pieces
3 carrots peeled, and cut into chunks
½ lb. smoked fully cooked sausage or fried bacon, optional
a little butter, milk, and salt

Boil the potatoes and carrots together until tender, about 15 minutes. Drain and sprinkle with salt. Mash the vegetables coarsely with a little milk and butter. Add cooked meat if desired.
Note: I have also used sweet potatoes instead of carrots to make this colorful dish.

Twice-baked Potatoes

I've lost my recipe, but I remember basically how to make them.

Bake 6 baking potatoes. When cool, slice into two halves, scoop out the insides and reserve for next step. Mix the scooped-out potato filling with a can of evaporated milk—5-8 ounces. Add 1-2 tablespoons of dried, minced onion and ½ cup of grated cheddar cheese. Place the filling back in the shells and bake them at 375 degrees until hot and the cheese has melted.

Prayer:
Thank you for Nigerian yams, Yukon golds, and sweet potatoes.

25

Cracking Open Eggs

"Probably one of the most private things in the world is an egg until it is broken."
—MFK Fisher

When I was a child in the Pacific Northwest, my parents moved from a small town to a dairy farm. In addition to having a herd of cows, they also began a chicken business. Dad prepared for their arrival, searching for any openings or scratching in the chicken coop that might indicate that foxes had been digging holes near its foundation. When the tiny fluffy chicks were delivered from the hatchery to our chicken coop, it was like Christmas. Dad constructed two large circles of walled fencing a few feet high that contained them so they couldn't roam around on the whole floor of the coop. They didn't need much space, and the close quarters would keep them warmer. From the ceiling, large brooders with warm lights hovered above them like spaceships. I'm sure it wasn't the same as snuggling under their mothers' wings, but it was warm enough to protect them until they grew into pullets. Sounds of cheeping filled the coop. I could just reach over the top of the short walls and touch their downy bodies before they scooted away.

When they grew older and stronger, Dad removed the two circles that had enclosed them and the brooders overhead. By this time the birds were not peeping or cheeping but clucking and squawking. When the hens were ready to lay eggs, my dad, being very good at carpentry, built houses on stilts at one end of the coop for the laying hens. When the hens went into the holes, each was in an individual apartment with a separate opening, so the chickens would have a private place to lay their eggs. One day I neglected looking in to see if the hen was there and was pecked when I reached into one of the openings to gather some eggs.

My parents also made a yard outside the coop surrounded by—what else?—chicken wire—so the chickens could go outside in the daytime without wandering too far away. Sometimes Mom threw some feed out there, but they pecked around on the ground for who knows what, bugs, I suppose, and the minerals in the soil, even when I couldn't see any feed. Soon the ground developed a crust of chicken manure.

In the entryway to the chicken coop, there was a room like an office, where Mom placed baskets of eggs she gathered before brushing them clean. One day when I was still young and didn't know any better, I took some eggs from the basket and threw them over the wire fence to the chickens. The eggs cracked and splattered on the manure-encrusted ground. The chickens came running for the egg and pecked away at it as though it were ice cream. Mom came running too and yanked me away from the fence. I didn't learn my lesson the first time. It was so entertaining I tried it another time. Eventually, I learned why we gather eggs quickly after hens lay them. They could have a feast of their own creation anytime by just pecking open their own eggs.

When I was older, I had to clean eggs. Sandpaper was attached to a piece of wood and shaped into a handle, and I brushed, back and forth, back and forth until the poop was removed from the eggs, one of the worst jobs I've ever had, right up there with cleaning toilets at the county fair. People expect their eggs from store refrigerators to be spotless. I was not an egg-eater until later in life, and when I eat them now, I try not to think about what they looked like before the brushing.

Eggs symbolize Easter and spring when life seems to break out of winter and open up, at least in the part of the world where I live. Leaves break out of buds, birds burst forth from shells and sing, and somehow, long ago a tombstone rolled away opening up a grave.

Many times, when I crack shells to scramble or poach eggs and the innards ooze into a skillet, and I see that perfect world of white and yolk, I think of shattering the private worlds of eggs. When I walk and see birds' eggs that have fallen from nests in the trees crushed on the sidewalk, I wonder how many eggs accidentally fall or are damaged before they hatch or how many are devoured by predators—shattered worlds for birds, lunch for raccoons.

We are careful when we pack eggs with the rest of the groceries. Eggs carry the sound of comfort and fragility. We begin as eggs, refer to saving what we need for the future as "nest eggs," talk about "walking on eggs." Eggs don't bruise; they crack, and once they come apart, they can't be put together again as "all the kings' horses and all the kings' men" found out.

But growing is a process of cracking open small, large, and private worlds, worlds we can't inhabit again, as surely as Adam and Eve couldn't return to paradise after eating the fruit. Taking risks, developing, forsaking the comfortable and losing our innocence, all involve opening to growth even if we develop new shells. One world may shatter in tragedy and another open to beauty. Eventually, eggs in nests hatch or break.

Eggs have private worlds only so long. We crack them open, hungry for life—even its messiness. As Robert said to Sara Miles in *Take This Bread*. "You can't make an omelet without breaking eggs."

Winter's Spring on the Grand River

Ice on the river groans, cracks
white pieces break apart, floating
loosened teeth in a watery smile.
Chunks of ice crack hatching chunks.

Hooded mergansers dive among frosty cubes.
the small window when they dive in,
stark winter's black and spring's white
see them, already departing

Recipe for Eggs on Pizza with Red Peppers, Olives, and Spinach

1 pizza crust—I make a whole wheat dough in my bread maker.
If you have no time, purchase a crust.

2 red peppers
½ cup Kalamata olives chopped coarsely
1 tablespoon chopped fresh oregano
1 large red onion, sliced into thick rings
6 eggs
2 cups of spinach, coarsely chopped, or arugula
1 cup of Parmesan cheese

1. Preheat oven to 500 degrees. Sprinkle cookie sheet or pizza stone with cornmeal.
2. Roll out dough on floured surface 12 inches or more for a thin crust. Brush with oil.
3. Sauté pepper in a little oil for a few minutes. Sprinkle on the pizza dough.
4. Add the olives and oregano, and then the cheese.
5. Arrange the onions on top, keeping them apart.
6. Bake until browned but not crisp, about 7 minutes.
7. Remove pizza from oven and crack eggs into the onion rings. (The onions will keep the eggs from running on the rest of the pizza.)
8. Return pizza to oven and bake until eggs are set and crust is crisp about 6 minutes.
9. Sprinkle with salt and pepper. Scatter the spinach over the pizza. I have also substituted Romaine lettuce and arugula for the spinach and have added oven-dried tomatoes.

Oven-Dried Tomatoes

1. Slice 6 tomatoes in half and place them on a cookie sheet.
2. Sprinkle with salt and a pinch of dried thyme. If you like garlic, slip some peeled cloves in the tomatoes.
3. Roast at a low temperature of 300 or 325. After several hours, remove them from the oven.
(Plum tomatoes take less long to roast since they are not as juicy as some varieties.)

Note: Roasting concentrates the flavor of the tomatoes. Use them in the ratatouille recipe in this book, or in pastas, and on pizza. I've also made a salad dressing by pureeing them in a food processor and adding some salt and pepper and balsamic vinegar—delicious.

Prayer:
Lord, thanks for spring and opening us up like eggs to our world and its beauty.

26

Strawberries

"Strawberry Fields Forever"
—John Lennon

Strawberries, Saved and Savaged

Now two days in the refrigerator and once plump strawberries,
slump in the box exhaling, losing pointed perk.
I stem and sort into three—
Slice some for shortcake and cereal,
smash the softer for juice in a bowl making a sugary sauce,
pitch the rest for compost
like words, trust the heap to convert scarlet scraps to humus
make something of them

summer's suns to season next year's crop.

I don't remember how old I was the first June I went to the fields to pick strawberries. I think I was in junior high. My younger sister claims she was in grade school. Our summers were divided into picking: strawberries in June, raspberries in July, and beans in August. I knew of at least four major strawberry growers in the county who sent out buses to pick up local pickers, usually school kids trying to make some money. We picked beside migrant seasonal workers who moved to camps in the area.

When we arrived at the field, we received tickets, which were punched each time we brought in a flat of twelve small boxes of berries. We pinned the tickets carefully to our clothes with safety pins—proof of our earnings. We took a flat and moved them along the rows with small carts. I could earn a couple of dollars for a flat of twelve small boxes, and if the bushes were full of berries, pick twelve flats of berries a day.

After the initial satisfaction of earning money and filling up on all the strawberries we wanted (who knows what pesticides we were consuming), I thought the strawberry season would never end. When we had picked the fields of the Northwest variety, we'd walk or be shipped to another patch to pick the "Puget Beauties." I hoped for rainy days. Strawberry fields and strawberries appeared in my sleep, and I smelled berries mixed with dirt and sweat on my jeans and shirts. Every muscle in my back ached from crawling through the rows. I tried to find a comfortable position; there wasn't one. I saw some people stand and straddle a row, a position that never worked for me.

When the day was over, I soaked in the bathtub of hot water until it cooled and a dark ring of dirt settled around me on the tub. Before Sunday and church, we washed the stains from our hands with a mixture of water and bleach. We went through many changes of clothes and wore long shirts and straw hats. I dreamed of getting a job in a cool, clean office where I'd be dressed up in high heels all day.

My husband Clay says he went out to the fields at six years of age, and as an adult teased his mom for sending a little kid out in the broiling sun (though it was the cool Northwest). One boss placed a stick behind Clay to see if he moved down the row he was picking. Our mothers didn't talk about child labor laws, but they knew what hard work it was to pick berries was, so they rewarded us with good lunches. Clay's mom fixed him deviled eggs, which he traded for something else he preferred. My sister and I took cans of frozen pop instead of the fruit-flavored fizzy tablets we usually dissolved in water to drink.

Diversions kept us from going crazy. We sang the words to top-forty pop hit tunes played over and over on transistors some of the kids brought to the fields. As friends and neighbors sat squatting while picking the berries, a talkative mixture of English and Mexican strawberry culture developed. I didn't think much about the adult migrants who peppered the fields, or what they thought about us. Occasionally, they made it evident they were talking about us.

Other diversions occurred because of the particular nature of the strawberry. The juicy, red berry is an open and unassuming fruit, wearing its seeds on the outside, and is especially useful for messy berry fights. Rough it up just a little, and its juices surrender, unless it is shipped half ripe and partly white from somewhere where fruit grows in the winter. That type will not ripen in a bowl unlike peaches, which will often ripen though picked unripe. The berries we picked were ripe and shipped to the local cannery for freezing and ice cream sauce the same day we picked them. The fields with squat berry bushes growing on the ground didn't hide the pickers like raspberry or blueberry bushes did, so we could look up and see who had finished their rows, who was bringing in flats, or who was goofing off.

In the mornings, we were sleepy or more ambitious depending on the day, but by late afternoon we looked for any excuse to start a berry fight. We'd see a berry flying in the air at someone's back, and then another. Sometimes a whole handful of mashed up berries was thrown at an unsuspecting target. Most of us who took a hit would gather the readily available berries, mash them up, and fling them at the perpetrator. I remember one of the berry fights particularly well because of its more dramatic escalation and because it involved my younger cousin, Kathy, who picked with my sister and me.

The son of one of the strawberry bosses had a green car, polished from stem to stern, of which he was particularly proud. He parked it in the shade and left the windows open with a plaid blanket draped over the driver's seat to protect it. His younger brother, too young to have his license, had a cocky attitude that attracted the attention of my equally cocky cousin. They seemed connected by the way they could get a rise out of each other. The younger son had been teasing her and had thrown a berry at her after a spirited verbal exchange, giving her what she thought was justification for what she did.

After lunch, in full view of us and the younger son, she took a handful of mashed up berries and ran to where the car was parked. He ran like a tiger in hot pursuit of her, but she had reached the car. We saw her make little circular motions with mashed up strawberries on the white hubcaps and moving up to the car door. Juice ran down the side of the car. By this time everyone was roaring with laughter, but I had a sinking feeling Kathy had gone too far. She worked quickly, and with some remaining mash in her hand, and to our gasps, slapped her hand dripping with berries through the open window on the blanket draped over the seat, then ran like a deer for the woods on the opposite side of the patch.

The tiger was motivated and gaining on her. At first, she dashed between rows, and then both of them crashed over the rows as if their lives depended on it. He was directly behind her with a handful of berries.

Then, all the while running, we saw him pull on the elastic of the back of her pants, drop the berry mash down her pants, and slap her behind. Those of us witnessing it laughed long and hard. The incident provided a welcome relief from the monotony. Fortunately for Kathy, the elastic of her pants didn't give out.

I have seen faces washed in strawberries, and berries splattered on clothes, but unless someone sat in a pile of berries, most of us didn't go home with red berry "patches" where the sun doesn't shine.

In the Northwest this summer, I purchased a single box of strawberries for $5.00. I'm certain I would have saved money going to a U-pick patch, but I don't see as many strawberry fields now, and I've had enough of being on my knees bending over for the berries. Now more raspberries and blueberry bushes, which grow well in our climate, cover the fields. The strawberry season seems to last a few weeks in June. Everyone makes the best of fewer strawberries and a shorter season, and people who love strawberry pies and shortcake snap up the berries from stands and directly from the growers.

I wonder whether pickers still have berry fights, given the decline in strawberry fields. As an adult, I now long for the taste of a fresh Puget Beauty, but as a kid, I gladly threw away perfectly fine berries to hit someone on the back of the head. Then I'd quickly bend down to continue picking berries as though nothing happened, and the berry had dropped magically from heaven.

Each June I recall picking strawberries and the dirt, sore knees, and berry fights but most vividly remember the taste of eating fresh strawberries. I hope I do so forever.

Mom's Strawberry Pie

1 quart strawberries
3 tablespoons cornstarch
1 cup of sugar (I reduce this amount)
1 baked pie shell

1. Mash half of the strawberries with the sugar and cornstarch in a pan.
2. Cook, stirring over medium to low heat until thickened. Cool.
3. Place in pie shell.
4. Place remaining berries over filling in the shell. Serve with whipped cream or ice cream.
5. Serves 6- 8. Berry good.

Shortcakes with strawberries
(easier than many recipes)

2 cups all-purpose flour
⅓ cup sugar
1 tablespoon baking powder
1 beaten egg
½ teaspoon salt
1 cup low-fat buttermilk or yogurt
¼ cup (½ stick) of unsalted butter, melted, cooled
36 ounces of sliced strawberries mixed with 3 tablespoons sugar

For biscuits:
1. Preheat oven to 400 degrees.
2. Mix flour, sugar, baking powder, and salt in large bowl.
3. Whisk buttermilk or yogurt and melted butter in a bowl to blend. Add the egg.
4. Add to flour mixture and stir just until moist dough forms.
5. Drop 8 dough mounds about 1/3 cup each onto a nonstick baking sheet.
6. Using lightly floured hands, gently pat biscuits into neat 2½-inch rounds about 1¼ inches high.
7. Bake until biscuits are golden brown, about 15 minutes. Cut warm biscuits in half. Spoon strawberries over one slice and cover with the other one. Serves 8.

Prayer:

Lord, thanks for the taste of strawberries, their juiciness, and the memories they invoke. Keep us from wasting the food we're provided, but thanks for the fun of berry fights.

Picking at the Borders

We were serious as children, doing anything for a season. Kids bowed over picking strawberries, throwing them when bored, talking about what we'd do with the money, our *futures*, over lunches our moms made; the sons and daughters of *gabachos*, knowing someday *we'd work at desks and cash registers*, *we'd* be driving the trucks and tractors...
For now we are covered in strawberry-dirt mixed stains on our hands, faces, clothes,
hardly noticing brown-skinned Texan, Mexican men talking and laughing in Spanish beside us,
kneeling in the dirt picking rapidly   as though their lives depended on it.

27

The Milky Way—Cream of the Crop

I asked the waiter, 'Is this milk fresh?' He said, 'Lady, three hours ago it was grass.'
—Phyllis Diller

Adult food fights are about more than a few strawberry stained t-shirts or a few broken eggs. They are waged in political arenas, the media, and wherever and whenever we talk about rights. "Brawl" is the more appropriate term for some heated disagreements over food (Ebersole 2017). Even milk has become controversial.

When I was growing up on the small dairy farm, like many others in the milk-producing Northwest, we drank milk almost directly from the cow. The only processing was chilling it first. Today not only is the milk pasteurized and homogenized, the stores are full of alternatives like soy, almond, and coconut milks; some just prefer these; others shun animal products, and still others are allergic to dairy products. But where I was raised, raw cows' milk seemed the very basis of dairy farm life. Once the milk was chilled, the cream rose to the top and was skimmed off for whipped cream and butter. I cut my teeth on that milk. Darigold milk trucks rumbled over the roads on their routes to farms and back to the plants with milk.

Homogenized, pasteurized milk took the place of raw milk for health reasons just as organic milk is popular today. There are also those who want raw milk—once a way of life and now in style. According to a New Yorker article entitled "Raw Deal," fierce advocates of raw milk are in conflict with the regulations requiring pasteurized and homogenized milk (Goodyear 2012). The raw milk proponents insist that pasteurization and homogenization kill enzymes and bacteria good for our guts. They also claim that because raw milk is not heated or homogenized, it is sweeter and sometimes comes with the "whiff of the farm" a "flavor known to connoisseurs as 'cow butt.'" [42] I am assuming this is a good thing though I don't remember that particular flavor.

Pasteurization and homogenization are two different processes. Louis Pasteur discovered **pasteurization**, heating the milk, in the mid-1800s. The process-controlled bacteria and became widespread in the 1920s. While boiling a food can kill its bacteria or make it sterile, it can also affect the taste and nutrition. Milk is pasteurized by heating it to 145 degrees Fahrenheit for half an hour or 163 degrees Fahrenheit for 15 seconds. Ultra-high pasteurization temperatures of 285 degrees F for a few seconds completely sterilize the milk, so it can be boxed and placed on shelves in grocery stores. Health officials maintain the benefits of pasteurization far outweigh the benefits of drinking raw milk.

Homogenization is the process of breaking up the fat globules in cream to such a small size that they remain suspended evenly in the milk rather than separating out and floating to the surface. The cream will rise to the top of fresh milk straight from a cow when the milk rests in the refrigerator. A layer of cream can be separated so skim milk remains. Homogenization keeps the cream suspended in the milk for 2 percent and whole milk.

Twin Brook Creamery located near where I live in the Northwest does not homogenize milk. They also use glass bottles, a sustainable method of milk distribution. Owner Larry Stapp claims glass has the advantage of not affecting the taste of the milk. He also indicates that people who are lactose intolerant or can't drink milk can often drink their dairy's milk and wonders if it is because their milk is not homogenized (Harbert 2012).

The conflict between advocates of raw milk and health officials has reached an amusing pitch with advocates of raw milk in full fight mode, seemingly more opposed to the regulation of milk than concerned about health.

At one raw-milk meeting, a man claimed he grew up hating milk until he drank raw milk. "Maybe it tastes

---

[42] (Goodyear 2012, 33)

better to me because it's freedom milk. It just has a little rebellious flavor in it. To me, it's the new civil rights." Raw milk folks cheered as he took a big, showy sip and called out, 'Freedom milk! Freedom milk!'[43] At the same gathering, some people serving food packed their own lunches because genetically-modified food was being served—as the "freedom milk" man munched on a bag of GMO popcorn.

Washington State is one of the few states to allow raw milk to be sold with appropriate warning labels, in retail stores. According to studies, only about one to three percent of us drink raw milk, and fewer than two hundred cases of food-borne illness are attributed to raw milk each year. When I was young, I remember hearing about undulant fever, known as brucellosis in humans, which is usually caused by ingesting unpasteurized milk or some cheeses made from the milk of infected animals. In addition to brucellosis, raw milk has other bacteria, some which may be harmful. Tinkering with food has occurred for a long time, but consumers are no longer blindly accepting it, and conflicts are more common, more vocal, and more newsworthy.

Dr. Mark Hyman has entered the fray by discounting the benefits of milk, period. "Milk is not nature's perfect food unless you are a calf and should not be consumed in large quantities by most people, because it can promote weight gain, cancer, and even cause osteoporosis." He claims that low-fat and non-fat milk are even less beneficial. His claim is that the huge dairy lobby drives nutrition guidelines, and most of the studies conducted by the food industry are more supportive of the benefits of milk than independent studies are (Hyman, Got Proof? Lack of Evidence for Milk's Benefits 2013).

His views go against the grain—at least for me. Perhaps mistakenly I want to believe I'm healthy precisely because of milk and dairy products. We were told that calcium is so important we trust in dairy products; most of the time I have milk, cheese, butter, and home-made yogurt in my refrigerator.

What is worrisome are additions to food in the form of antibiotics, present in milk as well as meat. Again Dr. Hyman warns in a blog that of the 24 million pounds of antibiotics produced yearly in our country, 19 million are fed to factory-farmed animals to prevent infection which results from over-crowding and to prevent cows' stomachs from exploding because of gas produced by fermenting corn. Hormones used to promote rapid growth of feed animals are also ingested; they also produce rapid growth of girls' breasts and prostate cancer. We stuff these animals with grains we could eat directly instead of feeding them the grass they need (Hyman, Occupy Wellness and Eat-In: The Power of the Fork--Part Two 2013)

In a time of pervasive conflict, the terminology of battle expresses our pugnacious attitudes towards a multiplicity of societal problems including the war on drugs, gender wars, the war on poverty, and food fights.

---

[43] (Goodyear 2012, 37)

We read of "fighting" food contamination and fighting what goes into and what is taken out of our food.

Some people are lactose intolerant, and some people are intolerant regardless of what is added or taken away from milk or other foods. Strident beliefs calcify, and we become infantile, like children in high chairs with our forks in the air, insisting on our way. Most food fights worth fighting for could be fought more humanely with a drink of the milk of human kindness.

I look back at a time that seemed innocent when food fights consisted of throwing a few ripe strawberries with or without pesticides at the picker in the row next to you and hope we can resolve food problems as we assume the grown-up responsibility of insisting on unadulterated food for everyone. We are hungry for that and thirsty.

The following recipe is from http://www.ayearofslowcooking.com/2008/10/you-can-make-yogurt-in-your-crockpot.html

Yogurt in a Crockpot

Plug in a 4-quart crockpot (other sizes work too) and turn to low. Add a half gallon of milk. Whole milk is often recommended for yogurt, but non-fat milk works. I usually use 2 percent.
Cover and cook on low for 2½ hours.
Unplug the crockpot. Leave the cover on and let it sit for 3 hours.
Scoop out 2 cups of the warmish milk and put it in a bowl. Whisk in ½ cup of live/active culture yogurt (store-bought or from your last batch). Pour back into the crockpot. Stir to combine.
Put the lid back on the crockpot. Wrap a heavy bath towel all the way around the pot for insulation.
Let it sit for 8 hours.
It will not be as thick as store-bought yogurt. It will last 7-10 days. Remember to save ½ cup for your next batch. Chill it and serve with fruit, or make a smoothie with yogurt, fruit, and spinach.

Note: I have strained this yogurt to make it thicker, but I like it the way it comes out too, the consistency of not so thick pudding. You can also make yogurt cheese about the consistency of Greek yogurt.
Yogurt can be frozen, and the culture will not be destroyed.

Prayer:
Lord, we need some answers. What we always thought was good changes as we learn new things. Help us discern what experts tell us about our food, and may we make the right decisions about what is best for our health. Help us tolerate others' viewpoints while remaining uncompromising about the need for natural and wholesome food.

28

EATING AND FOOD DISORDERS

"It is fitting to eat and drink and find enjoyment in all the toil with which one toils under the sun."
—Ecclesiastes 5:18

"We are walking, talking expressions of our deepest convictions; everything we believe about love, fear, transformation, and God is revealed in how, when, and what we eat."[44]

While some are out about food in public, for some people private conflicts related to eating keep them at odds with food or from enjoying it. Eating disorders don't just happen. For some, associations with food can become distorted when food and eating are associated with comfort or to hide problems. Others actually fear food and don't trust it to nourish them. Eating disorders and food obsessions and compulsions can be miserable, serious,

---

[44] (Roth 2010, 2)

even life-threatening, and can be difficult to treat. The dark, hidden side of eating disorders may not be uncovered until a habit has become established.

Eating compulsions and disorders may occur because of the way we eat. Do we prefer to sit around tables and enjoy others' company? Or is that difficult for us? Eating in the community may not prevent eating disorders, but it's possible it may have something to do with alleviating them.

29

Eating: Public and Private, Hide and Seek Food

"You can sneak food, for instance, hide what you eat from friends and family, but you can also sneak your true feelings. You can lie to people about what you believe, what you want, what you need. And you can examine your life by either looking at the way you live or the way you eat." [45]

—Women, Food, and God

"Young healthy females, no matter how ethereal they appear in public, will eat like horses in private, especially if they are worked like horses too..." [46]

—A Cordiall Water

I've mentioned some of the inconsistencies and disparities related to food, like rich dessert recipes and dieting remedies being covered in the same magazines. The pervasive publicity and marketing of food tempt us to eat too much or the wrong things in the same issue that warn about health risks. We salivate seeing rich dishes and

---
[45] (Roth 2010, 165)
[46] (Fisher 1961, 104)

are chastened when we see the hungry and starving on our screens.

Pictures of food are all around us, in the streets, the media, and in advertisements, prominently displayed. Words about food are widespread online and on TV where we can turn on a channel and watch food being prepared: whirred, blended, pureed, and sautéed. We see recipes and the latest kitchen gadgets. As I was writing this, I saw a television advertisement for small carrots flying across the screen, urging viewers to consider these Bunny Luvs the "now" snack instead of junk food. Our grocery stores and many restaurants are full of people. Food is everywhere.

While food is advertised and marketed, and always in public, it is increasingly consumed alone as people eat on the run, eat at work, or eat while watching television.

Studies suggest that 46 to 58 percent of people regularly eat alone.[47] For many, this is a lifestyle,[48] but I have wondered if, for some, food has become associated with being alone, not having friends or family, or with privacy, which makes it more difficult to eat with others even when there are opportunities to do so.

In Luis Buñuel's provocative 1974 movie, *The Phantom of Liberty*, the setting is a dinner party, but everyone at the table is sitting on flushing toilets instead of chairs. As people do at dinner parties, they are having a conversation—except they are not talking about the food. They are politely and intellectually discussing issues related to the topic of waste and defecation. But occasionally a person leaves the table to go to a little room, lock the door, and have a meal. To use a bad pun, Buñuel, one of my favorite cinema masters of the absurd, turns our conventions on their heads. On the surface, Buñuel's ironic scenes in the privy appear extreme—as extreme as anorexia and bulimia—serious disorders of excess and starvation that often begin in private. But Buñuel's provocative film questions our conventions of bodily needs: eating rich foods publicly, almost flauntingly, and excreting privately.

As more people consume food alone, does this change how we see it? Some don't eat enough, and others eat to excess, alone. Joyce Carol Oates in *A Widow's Story*, trying to adapt to life without her husband, and grieving him, has trouble eating. She writes, "When you live alone, eating a meal carries with it an element of scorn, mockery. For a meal is a social ritual or it is not a meal, it is just a plate heaped with food."[49]

In college, I saw the girl who was eating alone in the dining room with plates full of food take more for later. As I mentioned in "Serving Food," my college comrades and I didn't know the words anorexia or bulimia. The girl looked old for her years, and sad. She took napkins, wrapped food in them, and stuffed it in her pockets.

---

[47] (NPD Kim McLynn, contact 2014) (Hartman Group, Sung, Amy 2012)
[48] (Forbes--Food and Agriculture 2016) Several studies are based on Hartman's Group study
[49] (Oates 2011, 149)

People didn't come to her table, and I didn't see her talk with anyone over meals. In the dormitories where she lived, food was plentiful, and there was the usual waste when students didn't finish what was on their plates. The little boy who slipped an extra potato in his pocket which I heard about while eating at my grandparents' home had known hunger and scarcity and took the food for survival. Both the college girl and the little boy took food secretly, but for different reasons.

Eating disorders are not the same thing as hiding away some chocolates from the rest of the family or eating out of the ice cream carton during a terrifying scene in a thriller and realizing that you've eaten most of a pint, though a habit like that can lead to obesity. Eating disorders are serious conditions that can lead to death.

Our perceptions of our needs are complicated. A person with a history of starving may always feel they must store some food away for the future, while a person surrounded by food may feel as though she can't trust food to take care of her body, or that food is what makes his body undesirable. Women, especially, bombarded with images of thin women and good food at the same time, struggle. Clinical psychologist Beth McGilley, Ph.D., who helps women with eating disorders and had an eating disorder herself says, "If you're alive and female in America, there's no way you have a perfect body image."[50]

Geneen Roth, who wrote *Women, Food, and God,* leads a retreat for women with eating problems and says about those who starve themselves, "If less of them shows, that's less to get hurt." But the causes of anorexia and bulimia are multifaceted and trying to correct what one sees as a flawed body image is only one cause.

Meeting one's needs for food is not the same thing as hunger. We use the word hunger to describe many types of desires: he is *hungry* for knowledge, or she wants to win the game so badly she can *taste* it. But words like "hunger," "taste," and "bittersweet," are associated with food, and food, in turn, is used to satisfy more than one type of desire. Food can become not just sustenance but what makes people feel good, hence the term *comfort* food.

Roth claims "our relationship to food is an exact microcosm of our relationship to life itself." As one of the retreat participants says, "everything we believe about our lives is right here on these plates." [51]

A strong relationship exists between those who deny themselves food (restrictors) and those who overeat (permitters), according to Roth. "Both types believe there's not enough to go around; one deprives themselves before they can be deprived while the other reacts by trying to store up before the bounty/love/attention runs out."[52]

---

[50] (Novotney 2010)
[51] (Roth 2010, 12)
[52] (Roth 2010, 150)

She claims "women turn to food when they are not hungry because they are hungry for something they can't name: a connection to what is beyond the concerns of daily life. Something deathless, something sacred"[53] or as Anne LaMott writes in *Help, Thanks, Wow*, "You're not hungry for cocoa butter. You're hungry for safety."[54]

According to Roth, "No matter what we weigh, those of us who are compulsive eaters have anorexia of the soul. We refuse to take in what sustains us. We live lives of deprivation. And when we can't stand it any longer, we binge."[55]

In stopping her own eating compulsions, Roth writes that she became "far more conscious of what she was eating without the distraction of the radio, television, newspapers, books, or even music, and eating with the intention of being in full view of others."[56] She urges participants to pay attention to things you've never told anyone, secrets you've kept to yourself. Do not censor anything."[57] It is the consciousness of eating that may keep people from overeating, just as suppressing one's truths keeps one from living truly.

Obsessions about food, like weighing it or counting calories, make it difficult to eat with others. Eating alone, unlike starving or eating too much, may not suggest a disorder, but some case studies seem to suggest anorexia begins when someone, often a young girl in her teens, is or feels alone with intense loss or depression.

Beth McGilley, the clinical psychologist mentioned above, remembers being 17 when her problem with anorexia began. Her mother had committed suicide, and she was leaving the comfortable support of her all-girls Catholic school to attend college. Her weight and condition were less likely to be noticed unless she gained or lost excessive weight. Her anorexia began when she was alone, almost like a secret. Now she counsels people in the underlying issues of anorexia like grief and loss, perfectionism, fear, avoidance, and a genetic predisposition toward depression. (Novotney 2010)

Some interesting work has shown that families can and have helped their children overcome anorexia. Parents who are most concerned about their children are those who spend the time to work with them intensely to get them to eat.

Peggy Claude-Pierre, who had two daughters with anorexia and wrote *The Secret Language of Eating Disorders,* opened the Montreux Clinic in 1993 for other patients. She gradually and literally fed her own

---

[53] (Roth 2010, 32)
[54] (Lamott 2012, 87)
[55] (Roth 2010, 37)
[56] (Roth 2010, 211)
[57] (Roth 2010, 106)

daughters back to health (Claude-Pierre 1997, 28). Her theory is that people with anorexia and bulimia suffer from a negative mindset which is overcome by replacing it with positive feedback. Although the clinic she began closed because of alleged serious malpractice, she seems to have been instrumental in and somewhat successful at curing some patients (Claude-Pierre 1997, 133). The clinical treatment approach involved staying close to the patient at all times, so there was a high ratio of care workers per patient. Patients were not allowed to eat secretly where they could hide food or use laxatives to purge.

The writer Harriet Brown, another mother of a daughter with an eating disorder, tells in an interview about her book *Brave Girl Eating* how she helped her teenage daughter Kitty. The first morning of her "therapy," Brown realized her daughter was not just resisting but was terrified of eating. She told her daughter she would not be going to school that morning if she didn't eat something. The Cheerios grew soggy in her bowl, but gradually, with patience and persistence on the part of her parents, she began to eat (Brown 2010).

Another parent, describing her daughter as "defiant" and refusing to eat, stayed with her for every meal. She assured her that though eating seemed difficult, food was her medicine, and she was going to be okay. Eventually, her daughter picked up her fork and ate.

Kitty eventually ate the Cheerios with her mother's urging and insistence. The defiant daughter picked up her fork in the presence of her mother. Anorexia brews in the privacy of loneliness, fear, or depression, and may be cured at a table where those afflicted re-learn to trust food, eating with someone they trust and in the comfort of being nourished together.

Many people prefer and enjoy eating alone, often finding that paying attention to their food rather than conversing is a more satisfying way to eat.

I have often wondered whether there is a relationship between our food-porn saturated culture and eating disorders and whether eating too many meals alone rather than in a community affects our health. Some evidence suggests that control over what type of food is consumed, portion size, and nutrition all suffer when people eat alone.

Both those who consistently undereat and those who overeat may have food obsessions. For overeaters, food may replace comfort and desires other than hunger. According to one study, "anorexics 'eat' vicariously poring over cookbooks, watching cooking shows, and even cooking food for other people without consuming any food themselves" (Claude-Pierre 1997, 28).

Regardless of the complexity and causes of eating disorders, they are painful for those who have them, those who love them, and their families. We are often secretive about our deepest fears and desires. C.S. Lewis once compared the secretiveness of pornography to tempting ourselves with food. At one time, I thought pulling up a curtain in a dark theater and revealing a succulent piece of pork like a striptease was amusing. Maybe not.

I received the following recipe years ago from a friend. I have modified it several times, and it's an amazing versatile soup. I hope it is also a comfort as soups often are.

Gazpacho

¼ bunch chopped parsley
4 medium tomatoes
½ bunch green onions
1 medium yellow onion
¼ bunch celery
1½ red and yellow peppers
2 cucumbers
1 zucchini
13 ounces of V8 juice or similar tomato juice
¼ cup vinegar
1¼ large can tomato juice
⅕ cup lemon juice
1 ½ tablespoons olive oil
1 tablespoon Tabasco or chipotle in adobo
1 tablespoon Worcestershire sauce
1½ tablespoons sugar
2 cloves garlic, minced, or 1 teaspoon garlic powder
½ teaspoon black pepper

1. Drain and de-seed tomatoes, remove cucumber and pepper seeds.
2. Wash and dice all vegetables. (I use the slicing blade of my food processor).
3. Add remaining ingredients and mix well.
4. Marinate for 36 hours.

Note: I've added a dollop of yogurt to this or slices of avocado or some of my roasted tomatoes when serving it. I've also heated it to warm it up and served it with grilled cheese sandwiches.

Prayer: Lord, we want to be safe and belong and want to appreciate your gifts of food without all the conflicting messages and food addictions. Protect and heal those with eating disorders and help us eat in ways that do not contribute to disorders and food obsessions for others and ourselves.

Food: An Appetite for Life

EATING ABROAD

30

Hospitality in Haiti and Abundance in Nigeria

Most of our energy goes to making us more comfortable, not meeting essential needs and perhaps the most important work we can do is to distinguish between wants and needs and find something besides consumption to value.[58]

Most people interested in eating recreationally would not go to Hispaniola, the Caribbean island divided into Haiti, the poorest country in the Western hemisphere and The Dominican Republic, also a poor country, for the food. I have vacationed in the islands of Barbados, Puerto Rico, and Martinique, countries catering to tourists and offering all the foods they are accustomed to while they visit. Food magazines don't often feature the

---

[58] (Astyk 2008, 18)

cuisine of poor countries, or when they do, the restaurants' customers are not always the people living there. Clay and I visited Haiti once and the Dominican Republic twice and ate good food with friends in restaurants and in their homes. People with much less than we have shared what they have.

When visiting poor countries, it is easy to be paternalistic. Why don't they build good roads, install reliable and safe systems of electricity or solar, and purify their water? We may feel guilty about how much we have and how much we waste as a nation and convey that to people we are visiting. Sometimes we have trouble being good visitors where we are not the hosts. We are not the cooks or planning the menu in other countries, but guests at tables in homes and often churches. Making snap judgments we think might be helpful isn't welcome if we are eating together in community.

We went to these countries to meet the people, to see how they worked, played, and lived, and what their needs were. In Nigeria, we became partners with the leaders we met. All three countries have left an indelible impression on me. They are not safe or comfortable countries in which to live or visit. I often think of the people and our friends, and we watch for any news of turmoil. We were saddened by the devastating 2010 earthquake in Haiti, a country already so poor, and by the dangerous Boko Haram and the hostilities between Muslims and Christians in Nigeria. But we would go back to Haiti or Nigeria because we were welcomed and knew that if we traveled back, as friends this time, we would be warmly received, and experience life abundantly-lived.

We've heard so much about debt reduction and cutbacks; it's important to remember that austerity is not Biblical. In fact, the Bible is full of feasts, celebrations, and abundance. Yet, when we hear some politicians, it's as though some in society must be victims of scarcity or there won't be enough to go around. It's the opposite of the way Jesus lived.

For those of us living in affluent conditions, Sharon Astyk, who wrote *Depletion and Abundance: Life on the New Home Front,* calls for "a mass demand for less." When we curtail what we buy, use, and consume to live more simply, we may discover abundant living. Caring for material possessions takes time—time we could spend enjoying nature, playing with a child, or visiting a friend. (Astyk 2008, 20) As Oscar Wilde said, "We know the price of everything and the value of nothing." Perhaps what is truly valuable and abundant is one of the things readily available. That these things are more valuable than the things we pay for and buy.

31

Haiti: Light and Hospitality

Jesus said, "Truly I tell you, this poor widow has put more into the treasury than all the others.
—Mark 12:43

It was evening when our plane ascended over the glitter and neon of Miami, its lights, lime green, yellow, and orange, shades of citrus, like juices squeezed over the land. My first impression descending into Port au Prince was its few lights. I didn't see the few naked light bulbs until we were on the runway. The airport, dingy and run-down by US standards, bustled with people, and we trudged through lines with grim guards nudging us on with AK 47s. I thought of the Tonton Macoute, the police who terrorized Haitians under Francois Papa Doc Duvalier who came to power in 1959.

Once we made it through the lines, we found our friends and hosts, who were working for WORLD RENEW, then called Christian Reformed World Relief (CRWRC). It was November 1989, and we were in

Haiti because Clay had been invited to lead a conference for about forty missionaries from World Missions, CRWRC, and World Relief in Pignon Le Jeune in the Central Plateau. I sometimes wonder whether those forty people working in Haiti (and a few days later those in The Dominican Republic) knew what an impact the visit had on our lives. We had never been to such a poor country before.

Though dark, the streets were wide awake and full of people in tap-taps, the boldly colored taxis that are painted with slogans both in Creole and in English like "God is Love" and "Jesus Saves." Space on the roads is taken with a honk and a wave regardless of lanes. Our friends told us one road in Haiti has a sign which reads "la route dangereuse" not because the road itself has hazards but because of the way the people drive on it. Animals and people appeared suddenly along the sides of the roads in the lights from our vehicle.

The Haitians call all foreigners *blan* (Wilentz 2013). The term suggests the blandness of some of our quiet white neighborhoods at night, one of many contrasts between our countries. The acrid night air was full of dust and smoke from small fires, cooking suppers and burning garbage. We bumped and shook in potholes along a dark street in a four-wheel drive vehicle en route to the hills of Petionville where the wealthy people live. Our hosts say it is frustrating that the wealthy don't seem to care about the plight of the poor, and the poor often expect foreigners in development to provide hand-outs. Our friends discourage quick fixes and work to support self-sustaining projects.

After a good night's sleep, we were on our way to an airport and the small plane to Pignon, a town of about 7,000 on the mountainous Central Plateau, one-hundred miles from Port au Prince.

I had never flown in such a small plane. Luggage and passengers were arranged to balance the plane, and when we were all in our assigned places, the pilot stood in front of us. I thought he would be talking about when we'd be landing and about our seat cushions in the event of an emergency. It was not comforting when he led us in prayer before our thirty-minute flight. We were to be the fourth plane ever to land on Pignon's grass runway.

I thought of the American Airlines' pilot who, several years ago, upset the passengers by announcing over the public address system, "Let us all now pray to Jesus." He was advised to stay with the more comforting usual script that lulls us asleep while we taxi down the runway before we take flight.

While we Americans are uncomfortable mixing faith and technology, Haiti is openly religious. Doorposts, as well as taxis, tell of their religion. It infuses their culture. When we asked one preacher how often she went to church, she said, "Every day."

Their Christian beliefs co-exist with what seems to many of us primitive "voodoo" religion. Amy Wilentz writes in *Farewell, Fred Voodoo* that "Voudou, a religion that revolves around African-style ancestor worship and possession by spirits derived from the ancestors, is still practiced by the majority of Haitians in one or another of its immensely adaptable forms." She writes that "using the 'voodoo' spelling" which is negative to Haitians, captures the negativity that's been associated with this ancient form of worship by unknowledgeable visitors who show little real interest in it.

Once in the air, I conversed with the person next to me. I don't remember what we discussed, but by looking at her, I could avoid looking out the window and far below. I remember feeling like a leaf tossed about by every breeze we encountered. When we landed in Pignon, fifty villagers and their goats greeted us and the plane excitedly.

Our hosts in Pignon introduced us to people who proudly showed us the community development in the area. We saw grain storage areas and heard about programs to teach their children about nutrition. The local people identified projects they wished to adopt, and our hosts in development assisted them. We saw a bakery, and a market where rice, beans, corn, avocado, peanuts, and pineapple were sold. We were hungry seeing all of this delicious looking food, and soon went to the only restaurant in town, the GiGi Bar and Cine, which also shows movies on rare occasions.

One of the dishes I ate there was chopped up cabbage, like our coleslaw, only it was not served with the typical dressings. It came with catsup on top, because the cooks and servers knew that Americans liked catsup. It was a delicious and refreshing combination. I was impressed that people knew we liked catsup and wondered if we'd make them feel welcome by serving them foods with which they were familiar when they came to our country. I was moved that they served us this unexpected combination because they thought we would like it.

Clay and I took advantage of an opportunity to see the country and took a car instead of flying back to Port au Prince, six hours by road. Lush in places from the recent rainy season, the land was also dry and desert-like in other climatic zones. We crossed streams without bridges where women were washing clothes. Hibiscus and poinsettias framed the dwellings. We returned to quiet streets in Petionville. A strike had been called because the price for a loaf of bread had risen from 40 cents to $1.00, and people stayed in, honoring the strike. Our friends informed us that far more serious was the anger of the people a few days before when three people were beaten for requesting changes in the government. In 2010, long after we had visited, Haiti was devastated by an earthquake, but it already had a history of social as well as political instability, exacerbating its problems.

On the last evening we were in Haiti, we went with our hosts to a Vietnamese French restaurant full of international customers and some Haitians. The people seemed to speak different languages at every table. Except for the friends we visited, we did not see other Caucasians, though we knew they were here. Many missionaries from different churches in the U.S. come to Haiti. I wondered whether the people and the beauty of Haiti drew them, or whether they were attracted to a people who seemed to show them hospitality readily and whose passion for their faith was contagious.

The dinner by candlelight the last night before leaving Haiti, like the contrast from cabbage to caviar, is what we find in our restaurants too. I had pasta carbonara which came with an egg on top. I mixed in the egg so that it cooked in the hot pasta, and then poured some hot sauce on everything. I had not made pasta carbonara often before that time but made the dish frequently after the delicious version I had in Haiti. The meal I remember most, however, is the cabbage lovingly topped with catsup.

I expected to feel guilty about what we have compared to what Haitians have. What surprised me most about this poor country was its similarity to ours, one of the richest. People work hard, are resourceful, and have a spirit of hospitality. The land has beautiful areas but also erosion from deforestation. Unrest about the police and rising prices were pervasive. As we left Haiti and flew to Santo Domingo, I understood why our friends and so many others want to work with the people there. I also wonder whether the Haitians will avoid some of the problems of our country.

The Dominican Republic

Our next stop was the Dominican Republic. Haitians live here too, coming for work to support their families. They live in bateys, which are camps owned by sugarcane companies and their bosses. However, they sometimes stay in the DR and form new families, which weakens the family structure of Haiti. The work in the sugarcane fields is dangerous, but Haitians depend on it.

We awake in Santo Domingo in our friend's house to a din of roosters crowing, dogs barking, and motorcycles roaring by. Our friends tell us the Dominican Republic (DR) is "half-way" to Miami—between Miami and Port au Prince in its development. The streets are paved and maintained.

We accompanied a friend working in the DR to some of the bateys where he works with committees on development projects. He acted as our translator. We heard about the hopes and dreams of the communities. Our friend supported their decisions, even if they were not the ones he would make. The Haitians living in bateys work in difficult conditions and may become permanent residents, but still without the status of the Dominicans. In one of the communities, they were working on building latrines to upgrade sanitation and prevent disease. In another, they were building a park where people could meet in the evening, and the children could play.

We were impressed that our friend never imposed his will and ideas on the people living there. They know better than him what their needs are.

On the way back to Santo Domingo after a long day, we saw squatters living in a garbage dump on the north side of the city. Children were looking for food in the refuse of the city. We were naïve tourists, surprised at every turn. We know our friends are often overwhelmed with the poverty they see daily. We admire them for "teaching people to fish so they can eat for a lifetime" rather than providing the fish they could eat for a day.

In 2008, we returned to the DR. In some ways, the country seemed "more developed" with more cars, better highways and other infrastructure than it had been in 1989. This country on the island of Hispaniola has a higher per capita income, a higher literacy rate, and higher life expectancy than Haiti. Markets and grocery stores resemble ours and are full of avocados, bananas, and packages of cereal. The drive from the airport along the Caribbean on palm-lined streets is still very beautiful, and tourists come to enjoy the beaches.

But we were with people working in the DR. We went with them to visit leaders in Arroyo Hondo, a canyon with a river running through it that often floods and La Puya where some 25,000 people live in a valley, hidden by trees from the higher road above where the wealthier people live behind gated and fenced houses. If we had stayed on the road above, we would have seen the gated mansions, but not this shanty town, but we drove down the dusty road and crossed the river where pigs rooted for scraps of food in garbage strewn with debris.

On one side of the road in a dirt field young men played baseball hoping some pro scout would notice their talent and draft them. We walked among shanties in the settlement through raw sewage running through the walkways, a settlement that grows with more shanties farther up the hills from the river. Makeshift electrical lines siphoning power from the main line hang from some of the roofs. La Puya is a dangerous place of gangs, but it is also a place where a few courageous leaders spoke inspiring words to us about how they work to make changes for the people living there.

The DR is a reminder that some changes in a country may occur more quickly than others. The DR has more modern infrastructure—one type of progress. Where we visited, in La Puya down in the canyon, we found the very poor. One area may become less poor while another becomes poorer. The children may not be in the garbage like we saw the first time we visited. But perhaps they are rummaging in another dump, and we don't make a point of seeing it, averting our *blan* eyes. What has not changed is the will and passion of the people and leaders and friends we made both in 1989 and 2008 who help people in the Dominican Republic. We bear witness to that.

Pasta Carbonara

Serves 6

1 lb. bacon or turkey bacon, diced
2 tablespoons salt
1 lb. spaghetti or linguine
3 eggs
⅓ cup chopped Italian parsley
1 cup chopped red peppers
2 cloves garlic, minced
grated Parmesan cheese (optional)
pepper

1. Sauté the bacon until crisp. Drain the bacon and set it aside. In the same frying pan, sauté the garlic and peppers for a few minutes. Add the parsley.
2. In a large pot, bring 4 quarts of water to a boil, add the salt and the spaghetti. Cook until tender, stirring to separate the spaghetti; it usually takes about 10 minutes.
3. Beat the eggs in a large serving bowl.
4. Drain the pasta and while it's very hot:
5. Add the eggs to the pasta, stirring until the eggs have cooked in the hot pasta.
6. Toss with the bacon, parsley, garlic, and peppers, and either add cheese or serve it alongside.
7. Add freshly ground pepper.

Prayer:
Lord, we pray for those who live in poverty and danger, that the discrepancies between those who have plenty and those without enough may end and for wisdom to know how to help. May we be generous stewards in sharing what we have.

32

Snap Judgments in Nigeria

They are abundantly satisfied with the fullness of Your house, and you give them drink from the river of your pleasures.

—Psalm 36:8

In Haiti, foreigners are called *blan*, a Creole word which means white and often foreign. In Nigeria, we were a minority too and referred to as *Batauri* or "ghosts," which describes our white skin, not, we hope, the state of our substance. Yet in our wealthy country, debt reduction and austerity have nearly become mantras in the US news. Other wealthy countries are also touting ghostly austerity, economics, instead of justice and mercy. Austerity is not bad in itself, but it often adversely affects those most in need of resources while benefitting the wealthy.

Jesus' message and his life were rich with abundance. He talked about food, feasts, and celebrations; he didn't mention austerity. He willingly spent time with the poor, the sick, and others on the margins. What do people living on those margins—the poor, minorities, the sick, the disabled, and prisoners—think about this talk of austerity instead of conversations we should be having about sharing and abundance? It is condescending to assume that someone in need has nothing to give. As is the case so often, stepping away from our perceptions and habits in order to talk, eat, and worship with others in other countries and cultures can change how we think, and do so in ways we don't always expect.

Sometimes when I hear the gospel in a new setting, its truths, emphasized differently, leap out. I'm also thinking about how the story affects those in that environment and because of the interpretations of those in environments quite different from my own. When I worshipped with prisoners in a Michigan prison, I was surprised to hear how they interpreted a Bible story in the light of their own stories; they challenged my beliefs and assumptions. This also occurred when I visited Nigeria a few years ago.

A group of us from the River Terrace Church in Lansing, Michigan traveled there to form a partnership with a denomination in Nigeria. As we were riding through Abuja, we were warned about taking pictures in Nigeria, especially in the presence of officials, but when we were visiting churches, hospitals, and schools, many of the people gave us permission to "snap" away and then share the images with them. One morning we left for Mkar in Benue State, and our Nigerian friends stopped at a "fast food" kitchen where a few men fried some eggs and placed them on bread with a few peppers—almost faster than McDonald's—and delicious. We created a stir, and a small group gathered. A few teens in a marketplace posed, and I've carried their faces back to the US, along with many others. We told ourselves that the picture taking would personalize our partnerships with Nigerians. But Americans often preserve moments on film at the expense of living them out.

Early in our mission trip, we had dinner one evening at David Tyokighii's home. The scripture he read and his meditation set a tone for me as consistent as the tone on my camera that captured the shades and colors of my pictures. I closed my eyes as David read from Matthew 14 and imagined Jesus feeding five thousand people with a few fish and loaves of bread. The disciples, tired and hungry, must have welcomed Jesus' invitation to a quiet place. But the crowds followed, and Jesus began teaching them. It grew late, and the disciples wanted to send the people away so they could buy something to eat. They didn't think there was enough for everyone, and their inclination was to sequester Jesus rather than share him with others.

I often snap a picture without first focusing my camera or phone. If the object is far away, the resulting image will appear far off in the distance and perhaps overwhelmed by the foreground. As our Nigerian friends say, the image taken will be "small small." The disciples' vision must have seemed small small to Jesus. When he ordered them to feed the crowds, it seemed like an impossible burden to them. David cautioned us about feeling overwhelmed as we traveled to the Tiv land sites and saw all the needs of Nigeria. I soon realized what he meant as we saw the poverty, unemployment, lack of electricity and water, and inadequate infrastructure. Feeling overwhelmed with needs and problems sometimes happens here too.

When I worked in the Department of Corrections and saw many prisoners, I sometimes felt helpless to do anything beneficial for so many people in need. That feeling lingered when I worked for a literacy coalition. I saw students coming through our doors for tutoring, and their literacy needs seemed far greater than tutors could provide. When faced with such needs, anyone hoping to help can become burned out and give up.

The beauty and complexity of Matthew 14 is that it teaches us about organization, procedures, sharing, the resulting abundant life, and Jesus' outrageous love, all at the same time. We are meant to work out plans of distribution and work on them in such a way that all are fed. That's what abundant life is. It isn't that some people get fish and others bread; everyone shares the whole feast. Greed tempts us to keep Jesus for ourselves, to think there's not much we can do, but we are accountable. Sometimes in our frustration, we blame the hungry or needy and judge. We think someone is getting something for nothing, what they don't deserve, or that we are being taken if we are asked to give. The truth is that some people (meaning those with plenty) do not need to experience scarcity in order for others to have enough. Jesus' living generosity results not in affluence but in abundant living.

In Nigeria, I wondered what we could possibly do about the HIV/AIDS pandemic. But just as a camera can zoom in on a person or scene and bring it almost miraculously close, Jesus zeroed in on the disciples' judgments and limitations, and taught them abundant living. By dividing, sharing tasks, and breaking up the crowd into smaller units, feeding the people became manageable. So abundant was the food that there were leftovers—abundant life—both for those feeding and those fed. So it is for us when we focus on what is before us and enlist the help of others. Suddenly we have so much more to give (and receive) than we think we do. By taking action, Jesus made the small, large. Sometimes we think in either/ or terms of saving the whole world or doing nothing. Jesus didn't expect the disciples to live in these two extremes. Instead, he called them and calls us now to zero in and focus and pray that what is on the screen will show us a clear, intimate image of what we can share, and what we can do. Jesus' type of living abundantly occurs in community when we all have a part, not when we are trying to do everything ourselves.

Possessions like fancy cars, huge homes, and large portions of food are more about "conspicuous consumption" than true abundance. In her book *Depletion and Abundance*, Sharon Astyk writes, "Most of the important things in my life are items that are not depleted or in short supply," to name a few: "community, personal autonomy, satisfaction from hard work, intergenerational solidarity, cooperation, leisure time, happiness, ingenuity, artistry, and beauty of the environment."[59]

As we look at the camera images of the faces from across the globe and remember our partnership with global communities, our friends in Nigeria stay in our sights. We talked about needs, not austerity, and the substantial belief of Ephesians 3:20: "Now to Him who is able to do exceedingly abundantly above all that we ask or imagine, according to his power that is at work with us." Regardless of our skin color, we are all ghosts in need of abundance and the substance of Jesus.

Our Nigerian friends at work in hospitals, schools, and churches in Tiv land helped us see the true abundance of meaning of the feast in Matthew 14, and gave us the vision to see Jesus present in Nigeria.

Prayer:
Lord, forgive our limited vision and quick judgments. Thank you for opening our eyes to your outrageous love when you fed the multitude with fish and bread. Thanks for the abundance of your love in Nigeria.

Fish Rice Bowls

1 tablespoon chili powder
1 tablespoon cumin
½ teaspoon cayenne pepper
3-4 wild cod filets (or other white fish) or none at all
1-2 cloves garlic, minced
1 cup corn kernels
1 red onion, diced
1 red pepper, diced
1 can black beans, drained
Cooked brown rice (I used about 2 cups)
Lettuce
Fresh cilantro, avocado, shredded cheese, sour cream, or pico de gallo for topping

1. Mix the spices together in a small bowl and sprinkle evenly over both sides of the fish filets. Add salt and pepper to taste.
2. In a large nonstick skillet over medium-high heat, heat a drizzle of olive oil. Add the garlic and sauté for 1-2 minutes. Add the fish filets to the pan. Grill the fish on each side for several minutes, checking the middle for doneness (fish should be completely white and flake apart easily). Remove fish filets and set aside.
3. Add corn, red peppers, and onions to the pan with no additional oil. Heat over high heat for several minutes.

---

[59] (Astyk 2008, 237)

4. Sauté for several minutes until the peppers and onions are tender-crisp. Add the black beans and heat through.
5. Line bowls with lettuce and then layer rice, corn/pepper mixture, and fish. Add toppings like cilantro, avocado, and pico de gallo or salsa.

Note: This is good without fish too.

Small Bites for the Multitude

I wonder if, when Jesus fed the multitudes,
He gave them tapas, starter small bites of fish and bread
until they were full.
Maybe they waited the twenty minutes before taking seconds
to find they were no longer hungry.
or some knew about half a loaf at home in the cupboard,
wanted to eat it with the others,
Perhaps Jesus' words so filled them, they were satisfied,
or a miracle of food, showered them with plenty, enough for a feast,
we find.

FOOD FOR THE SOUL: THE LANGUAGE OF REST

33

Sabbatical in Iona And France

I know of no recipe for those who work too hard and long without a break except rest, and so in 2006, we took a sabbatical. Although Clay always had a passion for his work in the ministry and didn't say he was working too hard or too long, he welcomed a change of scenery and an opportunity to study independently for a few months. It gave us a chance to evaluate our lives. With that in mind, we traveled to Europe before going to Vancouver, British Columbia, and Regents College.

Our bodies are refreshed when we feed our souls. Where we traveled in Europe, we were not going to be answering the telephone, getting the mail, or responding to the other daily minutiae that weigh us down. This was especially true for the Isle of Iona, off the west coast of Scotland. Having reached the Isle of Mull by ferry, we still had thirty miles of single-lane road to negotiate to another ferry which took us to the Isle of Iona, one of the Inner Hebrides. Iona has a long monastic tradition. After staying there for a few days, I understood why so many people flock there each year for spiritual retreats.

Clay had led retreats for people in other countries, and now we were in one of the most remote, isolated, and beautiful but stark places we had ever visited. The island had few cars and no traffic. Perhaps it was this that gave us a perspective we wouldn't have had if we had gone to a place with traffic. But places are not sacred because they are isolated islands. The San Juan Islands here in Northwest Washington are beautiful; some of them seem remote too. Iona's history and concern about justice helped give a mysteriousness that drew us as it has drawn so many pilgrims before.

Islands or retreats are not the only places to recover. We can find sacred places anywhere. Eating at tables in other countries, we experience the sacred and are blessed.

34

Soul Food on Iona

Earth's crammed with heaven,
And every common bush afire with God,
But only he who sees takes off his shoes;
The rest sit round it and pluck blackberries.

—From Aurora Leigh (1856)
Elizabeth Barrett Browning

As Clay and I traveled on the A85, a typically narrow road through the scenic countryside from Edinburgh to Oban, I found I could not relax since Clay was driving on the "wrong," UK, side of the road. My brain refused to make the transition. I could see from the passenger seat out the window to my left that he was too close to the edge of the road. The road had no shoulders. After expressing my apprehension several times, a few unhappy words were exchanged, and we were both silent. Suddenly, a bump, and our tire went off the edge, fortunately just for a second, and then we were back on the road. (DIDN'T I TELL YOU THIS WOULD HAPPEN?) But my mouth was closed tight. We had already been through one traffic circle roundabout with a pick-up driver who tried to cut us off while making a digital Scottish gesture. Harrowing is the best way to describe being a passenger in the car that day. My heart—such fear.

We planned to stay in Oban only long enough to board the ferry to the Isle of Mull, and then park the car at Fionnphort and take another ferry to the Isle of Iona, one of the Inner Hebrides that has been described as a mystical place. But we were traveling on a Scottish bank holiday. Officials at the terminal told us the ferry was completely full. We had a reservation at the Argyll on Iona, but the next ferry didn't depart until the next morning at 10:00. We were disappointed but began looking for a room. Oban is a picturesque town on the water and a popular spot for a holiday. There seemed to be no room at the inns.

Finally, someone suggested we try the Dungallan Country House on a bluff overlooking the sea. We approached the beautiful Bed & Breakfast hoping they had a room and that it wouldn't be too expensive. We had no choice and paid for the room with a beautiful view, a plush bed, and a soft pillow, and warm towels. In the morning, we went to the dining room for a sumptuous breakfast of oatmeal, Scottish eggs, sausages, and breads. I ordered one more Scottish item on the menu, haggis (a Scottish dish made from chopped lamb's heart, lungs, and liver mixed with suet, oats, onions, and seasonings, which is packed into a round sausage skin and usually boiled.) Haggis is traditionally cooked in a cleaned sheep's stomach, but artificial casings are now frequently used. I suppose there are only so many sheep stomachs to go around.

I wanted to tell my friend Judy, of Scottish descent, that I'd eaten it. We had laughed at her one Women's-Night-Out at the church—the night of the ethnic potluck. The table was loaded with Chinese take-out, burritos, and lasagna, entrees that are such favorites in the US, we hardly think of them as "ethnic." A plate of pastries on the table had a sign. Judy, behind me, asked, "What are 'blanket bars?'" A few of us who knew, laughed. Banket (not blanket) is a Dutch pastry with a soft buttery crust filled with an almond paste mixture. Judy laughed too, and said, "Well, I bet you don't know what haggis is." I thought I knew enough to know I'd prefer banket because of my sweet tooth, but now I ordered haggis with my breakfast and was going to try it when there were other items on the plate, and I could skirt around the haggis if it was not to my liking.

Soon the waiter brought our breakfast, and since I recognized everything else on my plate, I assumed the sausage-like brown lump was the haggis. I told myself to keep an open mind, but I was disappointed. I didn't expect it to be so salty. Perhaps the salt covers up the taste of the haggis, which would be even more disappointing. Except for a nibble, I left the haggis on my plate that morning. Any word beginning with "hag" that describes food may have biased me too. Haggis must be an acquired taste. Note: When my husband Clay visited Scotland a few years later, he reported that he had eaten some delicious haggis.

After breakfast, we packed the car and headed to the terminal to board a very crowded ferry bound for

Mull. From Mull, we traveled the thirty miles to Fionnphort on a one-lane road with turn-outs to give way to people coming the other way. Along the way, we saw sheep with lambs grazing in the fields—plenty of sheep stomachs which could eventually hold haggis.

Finally, we arrived at Fionnphort, parked our car, and walked onto the ferry. While sailing west to Iona, no more than 15 minutes, we could see the abbey of approximately 800 years and our inn, the Argyll, which shared its walls with other buildings. When we arrived, the young man at the desk showed us the key to our room, and said, "It's not necessary to lock your doors. There is no crime here, but city people often feel better with a key. You may leave it here at the desk when you go out." I remember thinking not too many people interested in committing crimes would stay here, considering the effort and how remote Iona is. We "steal away," but what's to steal here?

Once settled in our room we looked at the inn's book of information about the Argyll. We had heard that everything we would be eating was grown or raised on the island—and the meals were delicious—but one traveler's comment in the Inn's book gave us pause:

> "But we have already committed ourselves by mistake to the wrong hotel, and besides, we wished to be off as soon as wind and tide were against us to Erraid. At five, down we go to the Argyll Hotel and wait for dinner. Broth— 'nice broth' —fresh herrings and a fowl had been promised. At 5:50, I get the shovel and tongs and drum them at the stairhead 'till a response comes from below that the nice broth is at hand...At last in comes the tureen and the hand-maid lifts to cover. "Rice soup!" I yell; "O no! None o'that for me!"...How our faces fell! It was, purely and simply, rice and water. After this, we have another weary pause, and the herrings in a state of mash and potatoes like iron. They should have been sent to the Prussian front as grape shot. I dined off broken herring and dry bread. At last the supreme moment came, and the fowl in a lordly dish is carried in. On the cover being raised, there is something so forlorn and miserable about the aspect of the animal that we both roar with laughter...It was so old it looked like it came from the Ark. To eat it was simply impossible...Nothing for it now but to order boat and bill. With more raillery we pay six shillings for our festival and run over to Erraid, shaking off the dust of the Argyll Hotel from our feet."
> —Robert Louis Stevenson

We decided every inn can have a bad day and one negative review.

Iona is a spiritual place, the site of pilgrimages. We, but especially Clay, weary after years without a significant rest to read and study, had come here for a retreat to begin his sabbatical. We bundled up, bracing ourselves for the cold breeze, and took a walk on the small graveled roads on the island, stopping to see the lambs in the fields along the way. One of the lambs, uncharacteristically assertive, ran toward us, and I fed the wooly creature some grass—longer but not greener—on our side of the fence. The few pickups and tractors we saw were mostly on the scattered farms on the island, so there were no distractions from traffic. In spite of the beauty of this wild and somewhat austere island, walking in the cold wind sapped our energy, and we returned to the hotel to take naps.

After the hassles of traveling, I was glad to be here but didn't feel very spiritual, even on Iona. An hour before dinner, we read our books and drank wine by the fireplace in the lodge and watched a second ferry arriving from Mull. We were beginning to feel rested and warm. We had three choices for dinner, and although I can't remember what we had, it was delicious. I felt more spiritual after the wine and that dinner. As MFK Fisher says, "Most bereaved souls crave nourishment more tangible than prayers: they want a steak." [60]

After dinner, we walked to the abbey for the service of silence, listening, and music at 9:00 PM, and after the service walked back to our room to sleep. Breakfast was another grand meal, and more naps, reading, and services at the abbey followed. We walked around the older buildings—ruined churches, convent museums, and a graveyard. Like the waves slapping the rocks on shore, the rhythms of Iona washed over us. One of our last services at the abbey had a powerful theme of peace and justice. At one point the leader said, "Every three seconds a child dies of poverty," and a gong was struck three times at second intervals. We sang the familiar Iona hymns, content to be in the wooden pews of the abbey while a haunting wind blew outside reminding us of hungry children, injustice, and war.

Peacefulness settled over us quickly as we became immersed in the land and sea of Iona, a truly awesome place. But few of us can live in such splendor for long.

Annie Dillard tells of watching a total eclipse of the sun on the hills of Yakima. She heard others scream when the moon passed over the sun, and writes with wonder, "the second before the sun went out we saw a wall of dark shadow come speeding at us…like thunder. It roared up the valley. It slammed our hill and knocked us out. It was the monstrous swift shadow cone of the moon. I have since read that this wave of shadow, 195 miles wide, moves 1,800 miles an hour, hauling darkness like plague behind it."[61] But later at breakfast, she thinks about the difference between mind and body. "The mind wants to know all the world, and all eternity, and God. The mind's sidekick, however, will settle for two eggs over easy."[62]

---

[60] (Fisher, most_bereaved_souls_crave_nourishment_more_tangible. Dictionary.com. Columbia World of Quotations. Columbia University Press, 1996. http://quotes.dictionary.com/most_bereaved_souls_crave_nourishment_more_tangible (accessed: March 27, 2014) 1949)
[61] (Dillard 1982, 100)
[62] (Dillard 1982, 99)

I wondered if I could live here at Iona or in a monastery, reading, writing, walking, contemplating, and maybe making some bread. Perhaps by escaping here, I would be more likely to experience God than in busy places where I am easily distracted. But God is on the move, and not necessarily in churches or other places of my choosing. God may resist the times I choose and the locales I designate and may frequent wretched places too, dwelling on the margins in ghettos, prisons, and war-torn countries and places where I may not want to be. As enamored as I am with the places and experiences that seem like heaven on earth to me, God is everywhere. As Daniel Taylor writes *In Search of Sacred Places*, "God is not any more or less on Iona than in my garage."[63] By coming here, we don't escape death, disease, and temptation that accompany us wherever we are. Columba, the Irish monk who came to Iona with a band of other monks on a pilgrimage, found we are not more likely to find God in Iona or escape from who we are.

While I was a guest at Iona, I read Rowan Williams,' *The Truce of God*, which cautions us about romanticizing the monastic life. "It is a difficult life," and has been referred to as "going into battle" (Williams 1983). Reaching for God or seeking a transformation, or being more spiritual only seemed easier in this idyllic setting than in a garage.

Those who live the monastic life struggle with burdens of discipline and discipleship. In fact, those who look for God on high mountains, isolated and away from people, find the oxygen-thin and hard to breathe. Jesus came down to us. When he went to the mountain heights alone, he experienced temptations. We were meant to be here. A plate of eggs with haggis on the side or driving through the country may be holy too, if we are willing to see the sacred in the ordinary.

We had spent only a few days in Iona. The morning we boarded the ferry back to Mull was stormy. We carried our luggage to the gangplank where waves splashed over it and tried to time our steps to avoid the high waves rolling over our path onto the ferry. My timing was not good; my leather shoes got soaked in salt water and took two days to dry.

I began and ended my Iona journey with salt—the salt of haggis and the salt water soaking my shoes, as though I had been seasoned and readied to enter the work world. In between the haggis and soaked shoes was a brief time of relaxation, contemplation, and good meals. I wanted to leave Iona a renewed and better person and almost believed it until we were in our rental car where I was back to clenching my teeth, closing my eyes, and trying not to grumble at the person driving, who was doing well and thought I was quite devilish.

---

[63] (Taylor 2011, 11)

White Chocolate and Blackberry Clafoutis

1 cup fresh or frozen blackberries (or raspberries)
¾ stick of butter
1 cup of self-rising flour
⅔ cup of almond meal
3 eggs
2 tablespoons thick cream
¼ lb. good white chocolate such as Lindt's
½ cup sugar

1. Preheat the oven to 400 F and grease and sugar dust a baking dish. (I've used a large pie plate.)
2. Place flour, almond meal, sugar, and butter in the food processor and process for 10-15 seconds or until mixture resembles fine breadcrumbs.
3. Add the eggs and cream and continue to process until well combined.
4. Pour the combined mixture into the baking dish and stud the clafoutis with chunks of white chocolate and the berries.
5. Pop the baking dish into the oven and bake for 20-25 minutes. A knife inserted will not come out clean as the clafoutis will be a bit gooey. Serve warm with vanilla ice cream.

Prayer:
Lord, thank you for sabbaths of rest and relaxation, and for Iona and its beauty. Help us see the sacred and beautiful in modest, ordinary places too, realizing that you live wherever we are. Thank you for white chocolate and berry clafoutis.

35

Looking for Lou Pistou

Americans are just beginning to regard food the way the French always have. Dinner is not what you do in the evening before you do something else. Dinner is the evening."
—Art Buchwald

My husband Clay and I had spent an hour walking from the Splendid Hotel uphill to the Matisse Museum in Nice with only a piece of quiche from a vendor for breakfast before walking to the Marc Chagall Museum. After more standing and walking, we were on the streets of the central shopping area and famished. Air France had recommended a restaurant called Lou Pistou, and Clay was determined to find it. We searched on the charming streets and finally stopped at a boutique hotel to get directions. The people were very friendly. The proprietor scratched his head, and said, "Mmm, a small place?" We vowed we'd stay at his hotel someday. He opened a window and pointed down the street to where he thought Lou Pistou was.

We set out for the restaurant and found the place, tucked between two shops, with red and white checked tablecloths and seating for about twenty. No televisions showing non-stop sports hung from corners of the ceilings. Only a change in the linoleum separated the kitchen, which was considerably smaller than many of the kitchens in our homes, and the dining area. The proprietress, neatly dressed and with good posture, greeted us, but by this time it was 2:00 PM This being France, the restaurant was closing. Lunch was over, but the restaurant would open again at 7:00 PM for dinner.

Since dinner is often the occasion of the evening, this gives the kitchen staff time to prepare meals from what is fresh and available in the market. Meals can be different everyday or evening depending on what is available in the market. French restaurants frequently offer only a few different entrees. The wait staff will say, "We are having tonight," and then describe what is available and how it will be cooked. If you have a yen for a particular food or dish, this may not be your type of eating establishment. If you are open to suggestion, what's fresh, and the cook's creativity, Lou Pistou will please you. We made our reservation for later in the evening.

But we were hungry for lunch and out on the street again. Other restaurants in more typical American style were open all hours, and we stopped at one of them. In keeping with our visit to Nice, we ordered Niçoise salads. The salad was similar to one I make at home, but then with modern conveniences and access to a wide variety of supermarket foods, I can make most dishes at home. While Nice is famous for the salad, other dishes are also fixed in the typical Niçoise style with capers, tomatoes, and the Niçoise olives.

After a trip to Castle Hill and a beautiful view of the Riviera and promenade, and more walks, first to Jewish and Christian cemeteries and then to an older, lower, and charming part of the city, we were ready for Lou Pistou. Once again, the proprietress welcomed us warmly. I remember thinking that perhaps she had taken the opportunity for a siesta in the afternoon.

The chef, the late Anthony Bourdain, remembered when as a fourth-grader his parents took him and his younger brother to his father's ancestral homeland of France. The young Anthony must have been insufferable as he complained about the French food and ridiculed most of the culinary customs of the country while insisting on eating hamburger with ketchup and rolling his eyes when his parents spoke French. Finally, one evening his parents went to a restaurant but left the shocked Tony and his brother in the car for three hours while they dined. He began to realize the importance of eating a meal as an event. (He also repented of his behavior by eating all the unusual French foods he had shunned, including raw oysters and the stinkiest cheeses.)[64]

A couple with a small boy sat at a table by the window, and a man reading a book was seated across from us. We began eating the delicious French bread with butter while reading the evening menu. The proprietress

---

[64] (Bourdain 2000, 12-13)

told us about the entrees and was glad to translate. Clay asked about the sausage dish that came with tripe. I tried to warn him with my look that says, you won't like it, but he had already asked what it was. The manager pointed to her lower stomach and said, "er…intestine."

The gentleman across from us also discouraged him. "It tastes like the Scottish er…

"Haggis?" I asked.

"Yes, Haggis."

Clay ordered cannelloni with vegetables, and I ordered a monkfish kebob with polenta. We indulged in appetizers—Clay's, a soup pistou, and mine, a buttery little beignet. For dessert, we shared a chocolate concoction surrounding a scoop of vanilla ice cream that tasted like a truffle floating in a sea of apricot sauce.

The manager didn't make the tripe dish sound very appetizing when she called it "intestine." Tripe, like haggis, refers to the edible stomach lining of cows or sheep, but trash, rubbish, and even rot are other meanings for the word. Perhaps that's why we call ground meat or miscellaneous organs hot dogs. Once everything is all ground up, and that little skin is wrapped around it, who knows what's in there even when they're called "all beef" or "meat" dogs? Maybe other cultures would find the label, "hotdog" strange. I hear Julia Child again asking, "Who's to know?' If we had always called hotdogs, intestines…well would a sausage by another name taste as sweet? The beautiful French language often makes things sound lovely, and yet "degustation" sounds to my ears a little too much like "disgust."

When we're looking to be filled, sometimes it's in our best interests to ignore how meals are prepared, or the ingredients in some dishes. There's a reason why almost every culture spices up meats with hot pepper, just as there's a reason for barriers between the kitchen and diners, other than fat splattering the customers.

Lou Pistou, on the evening we were looking for authentic French food, met our expectations. The food, carefully prepared and delicious, was memorable. Even more so was the intimacy with the few diners and the manager. In places like Lou Pistou where we couldn't count on people knowing English, we longed for some conversation with people of this city. We could have sat at one large table, with the small family and the man reading a novel. The locals blessed us with their warmth by helping us interpret words of food, our common denominator. While we were in their country, we depended on the people for services. Conversing with them was a bonus. The tripe, like everything we ate there, may have been delicious too.

Niçcoise Salad
Serves 2

2 small pieces of tuna—½ to ¾ lb. total is plenty. (This can be marinated for 20 minutes in some soy sauce, a teaspoon of sugar, 1 small clove of garlic flattened and dry sherry, or rice wine vinegar, with a piece of ginger the size of a quarter, flattened.)
2 tablespoons peanut oil
1 cup of beans or asparagus, boiled a few minutes
1 small red onion, cut in narrow rings, rinsed in cold water, and drained
Fresh romaine lettuce or arugula, about 2 cups
1-2 boiled eggs, sliced
12 Niçoise or Kalamata olives
2 small cooked potatoes, sliced
2 sliced tomatoes

1. Heat the oil in a frying pan (preferably non-stick) until it's hot.
2. Discard the marinade and sear the tuna for 2 minutes and, depending on the thickness, 2 minutes on the other side, but leaving the middle quite rare. Let it rest a few minutes, and then slice it thinly.
3. Arrange lettuce in the middle of the plate.
4. Top with the tuna.
5. Around the lettuce arrange the eggs, tomatoes, olives, beans or asparagus, and potatoes, keeping them separate. Sprinkle onions on top.
6. Mix together 1 tablespoon of Dijon mustard and 1 tablespoon of wine vinegar, and then slowly add ¼ cup of olive oil. Drizzle over the vegetables and season with salt and freshly ground pepper.

This is good with some crusty French bread.

Polenta
(6 servings)

1½ cups water
1 cup yellow cornmeal
2½ cups canned low-salt vegetarian or chicken broth
1 cup grated Parmesan cheese
¼ cup milk (yogurt works too)
1 tablespoons butter.

1. Combine water and cornmeal in a small bowl.
2. Bring broth to boil in a heavy large saucepan. Gradually add cornmeal mixture, stirring until well blended.
3. Reduce heat to low and simmer until polenta thickens, stirring occasionally, about 15 minutes.
4. Mix in ½ cup cheese, cream, and butter.
5. Season to taste with salt and pepper.
6. Transfer polenta to a serving bowl.
7. Sprinkle with remaining ½ cup cheese.

Note: I have doubled and tripled this. Leftover polenta is stiff; cut it in serving pieces or scoop it out of the bowl. It's delicious with sautéed garlic, onions, and peppers. Add some fresh tomatoes, olives, or cheese on top.

36

Lunch at Versailles: Let Us Eat Cake

"All knives and forks were working away at a rate that was quite alarming; very few words were spoken; and everybody seemed to eat his utmost, in self-defense, as if a famine were expected to set in before breakfast-time to-morrow morning, and it had become high time to assert the first law of nature."
—Charles Dickens (on American dining)

We stood in a long line in a drizzle to get our tickets at Versailles, long enough to look at the outside of the immense palatial buildings ahead that pictures never quite capture. Although it is not likely that Marie Antoinette actually said, "Let them eat cake"—she is one of many who are alleged to have said it—we grumbled while in line that these buildings had been built on the backs of the poor. The plantations in the south and the buildings in Washington D.C. built by slaves along with other fine city structures today built by the most recent immigrants and others who are here illegally stand as reminders that we still use unskilled laborers for heavy, dirty work. But I expected that I'd be awed along with the other tourists once we made it inside to see the gold and mirrors.

We finally made it to the ticket booth. I already had to use a restroom. Once we were inside the palace, we also had a good view of the gardens from the windows. We wandered through the rooms, including the hall of mirrors. The opulence and size of the rooms were astounding. Couldn't they have a few bathrooms in these "master" bedrooms? I began looking for exits with signs for restrooms.

The tour did not last long, and Clay thought he saw a door to the gardens. We went out to tour the gardens where I spotted a guard. He would know where a bathroom was. Yes, he pointed, go that way across the yard. I saw a small building and thought, yes. When I arrived, the doors were locked, and the small building looked more like an old sally port. It appeared that it was never used and painted uptight. Had he pointed at the trees and expected me to go there? Then I saw the opening in the fence.

I slipped through into another world like Alice in Wonderland. I was on an ordinary street, a sharp contrast to the Versailles postcards which usually show the palace. To my right, there was a restaurant with several parties eating outside. I asked the owner where the toilet was and found it. Then I went to find Clay, whom I had abandoned. I motioned for him to come from the gardens, and we found a table outside the restaurant.

Three handsome young men at the table next to us were celebrating one of their birthdays, and we knew from the bottles they had been there for a while. We had our wine, but the waiter didn't come back, so Clay went in and asked for the menu. A skinny waiter with flair and some drama came out with the whole wooden-framed chalkboard with the menu du jour, and with exaggerated motions, plopped it onto a chair next to us, "la carte." The guys at the next table, familiar with this character, laughed. The waiter took some more time to come back, and when he did, I said that I wanted what the guys were having since it looked like a wonderful cassoulet. He shook his head rapidly, saying nada, no, nein, nicht, none, waving his hands back and forth, hoping we'd understand. They were out of cassoulet. He showed us his recommendations, and we ordered chicken on a green salad.

While we ate, we conversed with the guys at the adjacent table. After our lunch, they had a beautiful torte with berries, and champagne, and said they'd be honored if we'd share it with them. Our champagne glasses and share of the cake layers separated by custard soon came, and we waited for the men to begin eating, and waited some more. Soon they realized that we were not eating because we were waiting for them to begin, and they looked at us apologetically and laughed, "We're French. We take three hours to have lunch."

"We're American," we said. "We take fifteen minutes." They took a first bite, and we bit into the delicious torte. We finished before them and made our way back to the train.

Not accustomed to both champagne and wine at lunch we slept on the train on the way back to Paris. I dreamed about the revolution: how easily wealth is lost, like falling far down into a rabbit hole: and how a world of fraternity, liberty, and equality, where we depend on each other for what's basic, is the Wonderland and can be ours when we open small gates into new dimensions.

Berry Torte

1¼ cups flour
½ teaspoon baking soda
½ teaspoon baking powder
¼ teaspoon salt
⅔ cup sugar
¾ cup sour cream
½ cup butter, melted
2 eggs
½ teaspoon vanilla
½ teaspoon almond extract
1 8-ounce pkg. cream cheese, softened
¼ cup sugar
2 cups raspberries
or 1 cup each raspberries, blackberries, blueberries, or strawberries

1. Preheat oven to 350 degrees. Grease a 9-inch springform pan; set aside.
2. Combine flour, baking soda, baking powder, and salt; set aside.
3. In a large mixing bowl, combine the ⅔ cup sugar, ½ cup of the sour cream, melted butter, eggs, vanilla, and ¼ teaspoon of the almond extract with an electric mixer until combined.
4. Add flour mixture to sugar mixture; beat until combined.
5. Pour batter into the prepared pan. Bake for 15 minutes. Remove partially baked cake from oven and place on a wire rack.
6. In a bowl, beat cream cheese and the ¼ cup sugar and with an electric mixer until smooth. Beat in remaining ¼ cup sour cream and ¼ teaspoon almond extract.
7. Spoon cream cheese mixture over the top of the partially baked cake, spreading mixture carefully to edges. Return cake to the oven.
8. Bake 20-25 minutes or until top is set and edges are brown. Place cake on wire rack.
9. Mound berries on the cake, pressing some of the berries gently into cake top.
10. Cool 10 minutes. Loosen sides of cake from pan. Cool 30 minutes more.
11. Remove sides of the pan. Cool completely; Serve chilled. Makes 12-16 servings.
The chicken salad we ate was much like the Caesar salad below with cooked chicken added.

Adria L. Libolt

Caesar Salad
Serves 4-6

6-8 cups romaine lettuce in bite-size pieces
Slices of bread from a baguette, toasted. I like to sauté them in a little butter.

Dressing

¼ cup Dijon mustard
2 cloves garlic, chopped
1 tablespoon Worcestershire sauce
1 teaspoon hot sauce
¾ teaspoon freshly ground pepper
¼ cup fresh lemon juice
¼ freshly grated Parmesan cheese
3 anchovies (optional)
¼ cup extra-virgin olive oil

1. Combine all ingredients except the oil in a food processor or blender and whir until smooth.
2. Slowly add the oil in a fine stream until blended.
3. Pour the dressing on the lettuce leaves and add the pieces of toasted bread.

Note: This is good with or without chicken or anchovies.

Prayer:
Lord, thank you that we can eat cake and for small lovely places to eat, and sometimes, for a longer time to enjoy meals.

37

The Last French Bite: The Skinny on Eating

"The shared meal elevates eating from a mechanical process of fueling the body to a ritual of family and community, from mere animal biology to an act of culture."
—Michael Pollan

I treasure the meals I had in France, which explains why the last sweet dessert of this book is French. If you enjoy a variety of foods and taking some time to eat slowly and savor the food, then France, and particularly Paris, is a good place to dine. Chefs cook a variety of vegetables although traditional raw vegetables in green salads are also available. I wouldn't consider dieting for any length of time in France. But the question has been bandied about: Why don't French women get fat? I have seen books that answer this, but I have my own ideas.

Perhaps the answer to the question is more questions. Why is such a variety of foods prepared? Why do they taste so good? And why do we stay longer at the table to eat? Alice Waters, after eating in France what had been picked that day from what was grown (and raised) nearby, believed that a plate of food can change everything. The late Anthony Bourdain recalls all the complaints as a kid that he made to his parents about the French food they were eating only to find himself and his brother sitting in a car while his parents dined for a few hours in a restaurant. Eventually, he tasted and discovered what the fuss was about. We are hungry for a variety of fresh foods, and the time to savor and enjoy them while staying healthy. It may be counterintuitive but enjoying a variety of fresh foods while conversing with friends or family around a table rather than eating take-out on the run and consuming high-calorie snacks may not result in fatter bodies.

Now for the second reason some French women don't get fat: I have walked on a few streets in Paris with wide sidewalks and narrow streets, sometimes closed off to the smallest cars. The unmistakable message is that pedestrian traffic is important. People are outside the shops talking and walking on the sidewalks. I've been in too many areas in the US that do not accommodate walkers. Perhaps the French (and Europeans) are less sedentary than we are. Our automobile culture has spread us out—and spread us away from each other.

Possibly another reason French women don't get fat on their luscious food may be counterintuitive. What to eat and the act of eating itself are important to the French. Independent farmers and an abundance of small markets with fresh fruits and vegetables are supported in many neighborhoods. Yes, there are big box stores on the outskirts of towns, but people do not need to shop there if they live in the cities. Meals take longer in French restaurants, and the wait staff doesn't rush customers. They don't bring the bill quickly. Perhaps in addition to the delicious food and an abundance of good restaurants, they seem to know something about the slow and mindful eating movements.

I am a slow eater, so when I first read about the slow movement, I thought it perhaps supported my habits. Clay claims that I stop eating not only when I'm talking but also when I'm listening. The fork has been en route to my mouth on many occasions when I had to laugh about something someone said, and only later bring it back to my mouth.

But the slow movement also refers to a healthy lifestyle and offers advice we've been hearing about for some time: grow and cook non-genetically modified food, eat what's grown locally, and eat it mindfully. The French seem to eat and cook this way and "from scratch." When I asked one French chef in Avignon how he made his delicious sauce for his chicken fricassee, he laughed and said he got it from a can. "Isn't that what you'd do in the States"? He asked. He said he couldn't make cassoulet for me because some of the ingredients were not in season while I perhaps too readily make substitutions.

When Clay and I lived in an Avignon apartment for a few weeks in 2012, I bought a few cans of convenience foods like tomatoes and beans at small grocery stores, but Les Halles was a short walk away. Almost every good food, herbs, and spices were available there. A row of spices and herbs was on three shelves, layered from coarse to finely ground. Because I'm not a food expert, I did not know all the types of cheeses that were available, and we were at the mercy of the merchants until someone standing behind us heard our deliberations and asked in perfect English if he could help us. Then we tasted instead of pointed and bought our Comté. Les Halles made it easy to slow cook.

Of course, I generalize, but the French seem to eat meals mindfully, with pleasure. They may be dieting but do not seem to be giving up everything. Michael Pollan, in *In Defense of Food*, writes about Paul Rozin, a psychologist who showed the words "chocolate cake" to a group of Americans who recorded their associations. "Guilt was the top response" while French eaters' was "celebration" (Oh yeah.) (Pollan 2008, 79).

Mindless eating may lead to eating too fast, so the cues that tell us we've had enough food do not have a chance to kick in, and overeating may be the result. Geneen Roth leads retreats for women with eating problems. In *Women, Food, and God* she writes about the importance of consciousness of what we are eating without distractions like TV, newspapers, books, or music, and in full view of others (Roth 2010, 211). Some in the movement believe that eating with others allows people to slow down and enjoy their food—something I've witnessed in France.

Thich Nhat Hanh, a Vietnamese Zen Buddhist, has founded Buddhist monasteries where people eat mindfully without distractions of TV, phones, or tweets but also eat in silence. Instead of talking, they think deeply about where their food came from and the laborers and those who prepared it. In practicing mindful eating, they often become aware they don't need as much food as they thought, and the food they eat tastes better because they become more mindful of the flavors and those who produced it (Gordinier 2012).

I have been at retreats at a Christian retreat and conference center where meals are eaten in silence. I do not find it enjoyable to sit across from people without conversing. I could lose my mind with too much mindfulness. Eating with others is an opportunity to share laughter, talk, share ideas, and more importantly, an activity where culture is conveyed. Children learn to interact with their families and others while dining. Michael Pollan is right about meals as a site for community and culture."[65] But back to my question.

Why don't French women get fat? Well, some do. When we were in Paris in 2012, an advertisement was prominent everywhere on signs in the street and the Metro about a program that would slim up women. And I saw some butts in tight jeans where Béarnaise sauce or too many French fries had come to rest. But ever since Garrison Keillor's spoof, Café Boeuf on *Prairie Home Companion* and the maitre'd named Antoine, Francois, or Maurice, depending on the show, about an awkward American dining in France, we have exchanged barbs

---

[65] (Pollan 2008, 192)

with the French. In a *New Yorker* article, Paul Rudnick writes from the viewpoint of a fictitious woman who says about the superior French women that their secret is their "Frenchy" attitude. He writes, "The American woman obsesses over every calorie and sit-up, while in France we do not even have a word for fat. If a woman is obese, we simply call her American. If a friend has gained a few pounds, she is told, you are hiding at least two Americans under your skirt, and your upper arms are looking, how you say, very Ohio."[66]

    I like to think that deliberate and mindful eating is healthy though it is not a panacea for weight loss. And, yes, while in France I saw some upper Ohioan-looking or perhaps Frenchy arms. Eating abroad made me realize those arms are everywhere. Look to your own thighs too, ma cherie. I wondered as I ate in France: Does this country make my butt look big?

Easy Chocolate Cake—Celebration, Oh Yeah

1 cup sugar
1¼ cups flour
2 tablespoons cocoa
1 teaspoon baking soda
¼ teaspoon salt
2 eggs
1 cup sour cream

1. Sift dry ingredients together into a large electric mixer bowl.
2. Add eggs and sour cream, and beat for 3 minutes.
3. Pour into an 8-inch square cake pan, and bake at 350 degrees for 25-30 minutes until done and a toothpick comes out clean.

Or, if you prefer, try one of my old favorite no-bake cookies. If it weren't for the sugar, I could justify having them for breakfast. Perhaps I can anyway!

---

[66] (Rudnick 2012, 65)

Food: An Appetite for Life

No-Bake Cookies

½ cup milk
1 stick (¼ lb.) butter
4 tablespoons cocoa
2 cups white sugar
1 tsp. vanilla
3½ to 4 cups quick oatmeal, uncooked

1. Combine milk, butter, cocoa, and sugar in a saucepan, and stir over medium heat until butter melts.
2. Boil 1 minute, stirring constantly. Remove from heat.
3. Add vanilla and oatmeal. NOTE: ½ cup peanut butter may be added here for a more complex flavor.
4. Or you may omit the cocoa entirely, but add 4 cups of the oatmeal if you do.
5. Stir well and pour into a buttered 9x9 pan. Cool and cut into squares.
6. Or drop by teaspoon or tablespoon onto waxed paper depending on the size you want
7. Allow them to cool before eating—if you can wait.

Prayer:
Thank you for the beauty of France, its scenery, its people and customs, and for chocolate. Amen!

Bibliography

Astyk, Sharon. 2008. *Depletion and Abundance: Life on the New Home Front.* Gabriola Island, B.C., Canada: New Society Publishers.
Ayres, Jennifer R. 2013. *Good Food.* Waco: Baylor University Press.
Berry, Wendell. 1990. *What are people FOR?* San Francisco: North Point Press.
Bittman, Mark. 2012. "A Chicken Without Guilt." *The New York Times*, March 11.
Booth, Norah. 2014. "Don't Bug Me." *edible Baja Arizona*, January-February: 68-70.
Bourdain, Anthony. 2000. *Kitchen Confidential, Adventures in the Culinary Underbelly.* New York: HarperCollins Publishers.
Brown, Harriet, interview by Diane Rehm. 2010. *New Treatments for Eating Disorders* (August 26). http://thedianerehmshow.org/shows/2010-08-26/new-treatments-eating-disorders/transcript.
Bruni, Frank. 2011. "Dinner and Derangement." *The New York Times*, October 17.
—2013. "Malicious but Delicious." *The New York Times*, April 22.
Claude-Pierre, Peggy. 1997. *The Secret Language of Eating Disorders.* New York: Random House.
Clement, Bethany Jean. 2011. "Is the Willows Inn All That?" In *Best Food Writing 2011*, by ed. Holly Hughes, 256-60. Philadelphia: Perseus Books Group.
Dickerman, Sara. 2013. "The Best Food Lover's Hotels in America." *Bon Appetit.*
Dillard, Annie. 1982. *Teaching a Stone to Talk.* New York: Harper&Row Publishers.
Drouillard, Laura. 2012. "The Food Defect Action Levels of Natural or Unavoidable Defects in Foods That Present No Health Hazards for Humans." *College of Literature, Science, and Arts, The University of Michigan*, Spring: 61.
Ebersole, Rene. 2017. *Did Monsanto Ignore Evidence Linking Its Weed Killer to Cancer?* October 30. Accessed 10 15, 2017. https://www.thenation.com/issue/october-30-2017-issue/.
Engber, Daniel. 2017. "The Sugar Wars." *The Atlantic*, January/February: 40-44.
Epstein, Jason. 2013. "Food Tips for Christmas." *The New York Review of Books*, December 19: 65-66.
Fauchald, Nick. 2011. "A Digerati's Food Diary." In *Best Food Writing 2011*, by Holly Hughes, 167-70. Philadelphia: Perseus Book Group.
Fisher, MFK. 1961. *A Cordiall Water: A Garland of Odd and Old Receipts to Assuage the Ills of Man and Beast.* New York: Little Brown.
Fisher, MFK. 1949. "Most_ereaved_souls_crave_nourishment_more_tangible." Dictionary.com. Columbia World of Quotations. Columbia University Press, 1996. http://quotes.dictionary.com/most_bereaved_souls_crave_nourishment_more_tangible (accessed: March 27, 2014)." In *An Alphabet for Gourmets.*

Forbes--Food and Agriculture. 2016. *Table For One: Why We are Increasingly Eating Alone.* May 25. Accessed 10 4, 2017. https://www.forbes.com/sites/thehartmangroup/2016/05/25/table-for-one-why-we-are-increasingly-eating-alone/#7619b948616f.

Fromartz, Samuel. 2011. "The Production Conundrum." *The Nation*, October 3: 20.

Fussell, Betty. 1999. "Assault and Battery." *Books--My Kitchen Wars.* October 31. Accessed April 17, 2014. http://www.nytimes.com/books/first/f/fussell-kitchen.html.

Goodyear, Dana. 2012. "Raw Deal." *The New Yorker*, April 30: 32-37.

Gopnik, Adam. 2011. *The Table Comes First.* New York, Toronto: Alfred A. Knopf.

Gordinier, Jeff. 2012. "Mindful Eating as Food for Thought." *Dining and Wine.* February 7. Accessed March 27, 2014. http://www.nytimes.com/2012/02/08/dining/mindful-eating-as-food-for-thought.html?pagewanted=all&_r=0.

Groopman, Jerome. 2017. "Food Fights." *The New Yorker*, April 3: 92-97.

Gugnani, Divya. 2011. *Sexy Women Eat: Secrets to Eating What You Want and Still Looking Fabulous.* New York: Harper.

Hadley, Tessa. 2013. "Experience." *The New Yorker*, January 21: 58-65.

Hamilton, Gabrielle. 2011. *Blood, Bones, and Butter.* New York: Random House.

Harbert, Jessica. 2012. "Twin Brook Creamery: By the glass bottle." *Grow Northwest.* December 1. Accessed March 19, 2014. http://www.grownorthwest.com/2012/12/twin-brook-creamery-by-the-glass-bottle/.

Harjo, Joy. 1994. "The World Begins at a Table." In *The Woman Who Fell From the Sky*. W.W. Norton and Company, Inc.

Hartman Group, Sung, Amy. 2012. "Healthy Snacking and Social Eating as an Obesity Solution." *Heartbeat Newsletter.* 10 3. Accessed September 19, 2017. https://www.hartman-group.com/hartbeat/444/healthy-snacking-and-social-eating-as-an-obesity-solution.

Huber, Bridget. 2011. "Walmart's Fresh Food Makeover." *The Nation*, 10 3: 22-24.

Hyman, Mark. 2013. "Got Proof? Lack of Evidence for Milk's Benefits." *DrHyman.com.* July 7. Accessed July 8, 2013. http://drhyman.com/blog/2013/07/05/got-proof-lack-of-evidence-for-milks-benefits/.

—2013. "Occupy Wellness and Eat-In: The Power of the Fork--Part Two." *DrHyman.com.* April 4. Accessed March 19, 2014. http://drhyman.com/blog/2013/03/15/occupy-wellness-and-eat-in-the-power-of-the-fork-part-two/.

Jayaraman, Saru. 2017. *The Future of Food: How do we build a just, sustainable food system?* October 30. Accessed 10 15, 2017. https://www.thenation.com/issue/october-30-2017-issue/.

Kramer, Jane. 2011. "The Food at our Feet." *The New Yorker*, November 21: 80-91.

Krugman, Paul. 2013. "Hunger Games, U.S.A." *The New York Times*, July 14.

Lamott, Anne. 2012. *Help, Thanks, Wow: Three Essential Prayers.* New York: Penguin Group.

Lappé, Anna. 2017. *Danny Meyer Has a Few 'Tips' of His Own.* October 30. Accessed 10 15, 2017. https://www.thenation.com/issue/october-30-2017-issue/.

—2011. "Who Says Food is a Human Right?" *The Nation*, October 2: 29-31.

Le Mieux, Richard. 2009. *Breakfast at Sally's.* New York: Skyhorse Publishing.
Lee, Chang-Rae. 2011. "Magical Dinners." In *Best Food Writing 2011*, by Holly Hughes, 270-280. Philadelphia: Perseus Books Group.
Lehrer., Jonah. 2012. "Kin and Kind." *The New Yorker*, March 5: 36-42.
Levaux, Ari. 2011. "Chow: Hard to Swallow." *Cascadia Weekly*, December 28: 30-31.
Levine, Ketzel. 2008. *Lab-Grown Meat a Reality, But Who Will Eat It?* Health and Science--radio, Washington D.C: National Public Radio.
Lieberman, Trudy. 2013. "The Real Hunger Games." *The Nation* 12-17.
MacFarquhar, Larissa. 2008. "Chef on the Edge." *The New Yorker*, March 24: 58.
Miles, Sara. 2007. *Take This Bread.* New York: Ballantine Books (an imprint of Random House Publishing Group).
Muhlke, Christine. 2012. "When Rene Redzepi Cooks at Home: The Forager at Rest." *Bon Appetit*, March: 94-105.
Myers, Amy M.D. 2013. "This Is Your Gut on Gluten." *Huffington Post.* August 6. Accessed January 27, 2014. http://www.huffingtonpost.com/amy-myers-md-/effects-of-gluten-on-the-body_b_3672275.html.
Myhrvold, Nathan. 2014. "The Art and Science of Bread." *www.newyorker.com.* 11 03. Accessed May 24, 2017. http://www.newyorker.com/magazine/2014/11/03/grain.
Novotney, Amy. 2010. "Feeding the Soul." *American Psychological Association.* March. Accessed May 3, 2010. http://www.apa.org/monitor/2010/03/eating-disorders.aspx.
NPD Kim McLynn, contact. 2014. "Consumers are alone over half of eating occasions." *The NPD Group, Inc.* August 7. Accessed September 19, 2017. https://www.npd.com/wps/portal/npd/us/news/press-releases/consumers-are-alone-over-half-of-eating-occasions-as-a-result-of-changing-lifestyles-and-more-single-person-households-reports-npd/.
Oates, Joyce Carol. 2011. *A Widow's Story.* New York: HarperCollins Publishers.
Osnos, Evan. 2014. "Chemical Valley." *The New Yorker*, April 7: 38-49.
Oxfam. 2013. "7 Photos That Reveal What Families Eat In One Week." *Oxfam America.* Spring. Accessed 2013. oxfamamerica.org/sevenphotos.
Pollan, Michael. 2008. *In Defense of Food: An Eater's Manifesto.* New York: The Penguin Press.
n.d. "Potlatch." *Wikipedia.* Accessed November 5, 2013.
Pugh, Derek. 2013. "The 10 Farm Subsidy Recipients Who Voted to Cut Food Stamps." *Campaign for America's Future.* September 20. Accessed March 12, 2014. http://ourfuture.org/20130920/the-10-farm-subsidy-recipients-who-voted-to-cut-food-stamps.
Ratner, Lizzy. 2012. "Food Stamps vs. Poverty." *The Nation*, January 2: 12-17.
Rice, Xan. 2013. "Now Serving." *The New Yorker*, September 20: 26-33.
Roberts, Paul. 2008. *The End of Food.* New York, Boston: Houghton Mifflin Company.
Roth, Geneen. 2010. *Women Food and God.* New York: Scribner, a division of Simon and Schuster, Inc.

Rudnick, Paul. 2012. "Vive La France (in Shouts and Murmurs)." *The New Yorker*, March 26: 65.

Schlosser, Eric. 2001. *Fast Food Nation.* New York: Houghton Mifflin Co.

Silva, Jill Wendholt. 2011. "Life In A Food Desert." In *Best Food Writing 2011*, by Holly Hughes, 147-151. Philadephia: Perseus Books Group.

Sorkin, Michael. 2013. "Drawing the Line." *The Nation* 32-35.

Steingraber, Sandra. 2011. "How we're poisoning our children." *The Christian Century*, December 27: 22-25.

Tarre, Marci. 2014. "Gather Round, Grasshoppers." *edible Baja Arizona*, January-February: 71-75.

Taylor, Daniel. 2011. *In Search of Sacred Places: Looking for Wisdom on Celtic Holy Islands.* Saint Paul: Bog Walk Press.

Thompson, Gabriel. 2012. "Work Till You Drop." *The Nation*, May 14: 23-26.

2013. "USDA Poultry Inspection Proposal: Separating Myth vs. Fact." *National Chicken Council.* April 14. Accessed September 19, 2017. http://www.nationalchickencouncil.org/usdas-poultry-inspection-proposal-separating-myth-vs-fact/.

Weaver-Zercher, Valerie. 2013. "Eat with Joy: Redeeming God's Gift of Food(by Rachel Marie Stone) Book review." *The Christian Century.* July 22. Accessed April 5, 2014. http://www.christiancentury.org/reviews/2013-07/eat-joy-rachel-marie-stone.

Wilentz, Amy. 2013. "Letter From Haiti: Life in the Ruins." *The Nation*, January 28.

Williams, Rowan. 1983. *The Truce of God.* London: Fount Paperbacks in association with Faith Press.

Wirzba, Norman. 2012. "Eating in Ignorance." *The Christian Century*, May 30. Accessed November 20, 2017. https://www.christiancentury.org/article/2012-05/eating-ignorance

Adria L. Libolt

Discussion Questions

Preface

Recipe: Simple Souffle

Chapter 1 **Hungry for Everything and A Taste of Fullness**

Why do you think the media encourages and pushes delicious food, often high in calories and at the same time advises diets and healthy eating? What contradictions do you see in the media?

What does it mean to talk about fashionable food? What is in "style" today? Why does this occur?

How do we judge what others eat? Why does this occur?

Why besides losing weight do people diet? Why are so many unsuccessful?

How are disparities of available food (and needs) related to justice?

What do the author's choices for her meal tell us about her?

What obsessions about food keep us from enjoying it?

Recipe: Chicken Marsala with Sage and Crepes Maison

Chapter 2 **Playing with Food**

What is the value of experimenting with food?

When does it have disadvantages?

How are we "prisoners" of the market?

Recipe: Veggie burgers

Chapter 3 **Foraging**

What is attractive about foraging for food? What are the problems with foraging?

Recipe: Apples of Eve and Apple Crostata

Chapter 4 **A Nibble without a Quibble: Small Bites—tapas, lazy susans, appetizers, small plates**

Why have small bites become popular?

Recipe: Asian marinade, salmon appetizer, tapenade, marinated goat cheese

Chapter 5 **Finger Foods**

How have we removed food from "our touch?" What are the advantages of having food produced on a mass scale? How do we keep food cheap? What does it say about the way we eat that we have hunger and obesity?

Recipe: Focaccia and Communion Bread

Chapter 6 **Sgt Peppers**

What have we learned from our melting pot of cultures? How have other cultures enriched our cuisines?

Recipe: Hummus bi Tahini

Chapter 7 **Middle Eastern Lunch**

Recipe: Taabbouleh

Chapter 8 **Beef for Real and Sausage**

Describe a time when you've taken someone's advice about food. Describe the circumstances when you've given others' advice about eating.

Recipe: Cassoulet

Chapter 9 **Turkey**

How does it affect your taste for meat if you know how it is handled in a factory?

Recipe: Turkey and a Dressing

Chapter 10 **Bueche de Noel**

Why do we do special things on holidays especially Christmas that take us from our routines?

Recipe: Bueche de Noel

Chapter 11 **Feeding on Advice**

Why do you think advice often accompanies food?

How does advice about food keep traditions alive?

Recipe: Ollie Bollen

Chapter 12 **Food Accidents**

Discuss a time when you've invented a dish accidentally, and whether it was edible or not.

What are advantages of inventing dishes?

Recipe: Moowiches, chocolate chip pie, and chicken soufflé

Chapter 13 **A Near Ruin by Ruam**

Describe a meal that made you ill. What were the circumstances?

Recipe: Ruam

Chapter 14 **Shaping a Signature Dish**

How do we shape our world by what and how we eat? How are we shaped by the food we eat?

Recipe: Surprise hamburgers

Chapter 15 **Luck of the Pot**

Why is there both hunger and obesity and waste in our country? In what ways is the industrialization of our food system a problem? (see chapter 9 also) What are alternatives?

Recipe: Ratatouille

Chapter 16 **Waiting, Receiving, Serving**

No recipe

Chapter 17 **Serving Food**

Why did students resist family style meals? What can we learn by waiting on tables?

Recipe: Tostadas

Chapter 18 **The Table**

Why does the author think that sitting at a table is important? What do we lose by not dining together at tables?

Recipe: Drunk Chicken

Chapter 19 **Waiting on Diners**

Why have we become more casual in restaurants? What are advantages to formality? Informality?

Recipe: Bananas Foster

Chapter 20 **Serving and Eating Free**

When has providing food or a meal been a powerful experience for you? Describe a situation of eating when a meal has been a powerful experience.

Why does Ahmed Jamal continue to serve food when it's dangerous to do so?

Recipe: Quick Fried Fish

Chapter 21 **Wildly Eating Each Other**

What are the dangers of eating wild animals?

Recipe: Pasta with cauliflower, green olives, and almonds

Chapter 22 **Memories and Associations**

Describe an association you have with certain foods. What impact did it have on what you eat now?

No recipe

Chapter 23 **Food From Heaven**

Why are some foods so precious to us?

Recipe: Mashed potatoes and Yam Salad

Chapter 24 **One Potato Two**

Recipe: Hutspot

Chapter 25 **Cracking Open Eggs**

Why is it that some foods are so strongly associated with memories?

Recipe: Eggs on pizza with Red Peppers, Olives, and Spinach

Chapter 26 **Strawberries**

What was it about potatoes, eggs, strawberries, and milk that had an impact on the author?

Recipe: Strawberry Pie and Strawberry Shortcake

Chapter 27 **Milk**

What is important enough for you to fight for when it comes to our food? Have you ever insisted on something related to food?

Recipe: Yogurt

Chapter 28 **Eating disorders—introduction**

Chapter 29 **Eating and Food Disorders**

What do you think the difference between an eating disorder and food disorder is? What are possible causes of eating disorders? How have they been treated? Cured?

Recipe: Gazpacho

Chapter 30 **Eating Abroad**

What negative assumptions do we often have when visiting countries? What is important to remember about eating in other countries?

What is abundant living? What gifts and riches do we have that do not involve money exchanges and transactions?

No recipe

Chapter 31 **Haiti**

What riches did the author see in Haiti and the Dominican Republic? What similarities are there to the way she lives in the United States?

Recipe: Pasta Carbonara

Chapter 32 **Nigeria**

How did the author see the Bible and particularly the gospel in a new way in Nigeria? How does Matthew 14 show the importance of organization? What does this tell us about how we can approach food distribution and other needs in the world? What mistakes do we often make when hoping to help others?

Recipe: Fish Rice Bowls

Chapter 33 **Food for the Soul—Introduction**

No recipe

Chapter 34 **Iona**

What moments in your life seemed sacred? Where have you been when you felt that you were on holy ground? What place? Why was it sacred? When have you expected to feel particularly sacred and did not?

Recipe: White Chocolate and Blackberry Clafoutis

Chapter 35 **Looking for Lou Pistou**

What was the beauty for the author of dining at Lou Pistou?

Recipe: Polenta and Nicoise Salad

Chapter 36 **Lunch at Versailles: Let us Eat Cake**

What is implied with "Let them eat cake?" What similarities were there to that era at modern Versailles? What were the contrasts between what the author saw in the palace and where she ate? What similarities?

Recipe: Berry Torte and Chicken Salad

Chapter 37 **The Last French Bite**

Why is eating in France so enjoyable for the author? What qualities of meals and French food are attractive?

Recipe: Two Chocolate recipes, one cake and one meatless—just kidding.